GOD AND BLACKNESS

God and Blackness

Race, Gender, and Identity in a Middle Class Afrocentric Church

Andrea C. Abrams

NEW YORK UNIVERSITY PRESS

New York and London

NEW YORK UNIVERSITY PRESS
New York and London
www.nyupress.org

References to Internet Websites (URLs) were accurate at the time of writing.
Neither the author nor New York University Press is responsible for URLs that
may have expired or changed since the manuscript was prepared.

For Library of Congress Cataloging-in-Publication data,
please contact the Library of Congress.

ISBN: 978-0-8147-0523-0 (cloth)
ISBN: 978-0-8147-0524-7 (paper)

New York University Press books are printed on acid-free paper,
and their binding materials are chosen for strength and durability.
We strive to use environmentally responsible suppliers and materials
to the greatest extent possible in publishing our books.

Manufactured in the United States of America

10 9 8 7 6 5 4 3 2 1

Also available as an ebook

CONTENTS

ACKNOWLEDGMENTS

I extend my gratitude to First African Presbyterian Church, especially Reverend Dr. Mark Lomax, Reverend Dr. Will Coleman, Reverend Dr. Itahari Toure, and the church members who participated in my research project. Your graciousness, candor, and insight made this project possible, and I have tried my best to respect the work that you are doing as a community.

I thank Dr. Peggy Barlett, Dr. Johnnetta B. Cole, Dr. Bruce Knauft, Dr. Tracy Rone, and Dr. Dianne Stewart, who each provided crucial theoretical guidance, support, and inspiration. With all my heart, I thank Dr. Matsheliso Molapo, Dr. Sally Seraphin, Dr. Riche Daniel-Barnes, Dr. Maurita Poole, Dr. Leandris Liburd, Amanda Hillman, and LaSherri Bush, the Sisterhood, who provided deeply appreciated friendship and love. I am also indebted to Dr. Martha Rees, who taught me to love anthropology; Dr. James Flanagan, Dr. Marie Danforth, and Dr. Carol Ware of the University of Southern Mississippi, who taught me how to be an anthropologist; and Dr. Yvonne Newsome and Dr. Brenda Hoke of Agnes Scott College, who supported my dream and helped me learn how to teach.

I would not have completed this book without the invaluable critical feedback and patience of Jennifer Hammer, senior editor at New York University Press. I am also grateful for the keen eye of Dorothea Stillman Halliday, managing editor at the press. Thank you, Jennifer and Dorothea. Thank you to my colleagues at Centre College, J. H. Atkins, Beau Weston, Phyllis Passariello, Sarah Goodrum, Endre Nyerges, and Robyn Cutright. I am also grateful for the encouragement and unwavering enthusiasm of my friends Eva Cadavid, Laura Hunt, and Danya Ferraro.

I acknowledge, appreciate, and adore Dr. Demetrius Semien, whose partnership, support, and love have made all the difference in the past five years.

Finally, there are no words adequate to thank my parents, Reverend Robert Abrams and Reverend Carolyn Abrams. You are my rock and my fortress. I thank my siblings Stacey, Leslie, Richard, Walter, and Jeanine, whose love makes all things possible. I am especially grateful to my sisters, who read and reread without complaint and provided essential feedback. You always believed even when I did not. And I love each of you.

Introduction

Sunday Morning

Anthropology of a Church

Eleven O'clock Service

First Afrikan Presbyterian Church is a standard triangle-faced red brick building surrounded by a parking lot, a few acres of grass, and several trees. Located in Lithonia, a suburb of Atlanta, the church is adjacent to several subdivisions and is the religious home of a predominantly African American and middle class population. As I walk up the four steps to the front doors, two smiling-faced gentlemen greet me, one of whom says how nice I look this morning and both of whom seem genuinely glad that I have come to worship at their church this fine summer day. I return their greetings, and, entering the narthex, I see a table upon which rests the announcements for the week, fliers for events throughout the community. and sign-up sheets for one of the Bible study classes offered on Wednesday. Over the door leading into the sanctuary is a black, white, and red banner that reads, "Invest in the First Afrikan Way."

The church has a modest-sized sanctuary with twenty-six pews comfortably seating approximately five hundred people. In the front is the wooden pulpit, a two-tiered choir loft, and, off to the side, a small ensemble of pianist, drummer, trumpeter, and saxophonist. As they softly play a jazz rendition of "Amazing Grace," I take my seat and stock of the surroundings. It is at this point that I note, behind the pulpit, a large wooden cross draped with a generous swath of green cloth, as well as a chain of iron from which hangs a multihued fabric ankh, an African icon considered the original cross and the symbolic representation of both physical and eternal life. Absent from the sanctuary walls, painted in warm oatmeal, are the usual pictures and stained-glass images of Jesus and the saints. Rather, the walls are adorned with several large African masks, a portrait of an old and serene black grandmother, and a coffee-colored Gabriel with elaborate wings and a faint resemblance to Denzel Washington, the actor.

Among my companions in the sanctuary are men with low-cut hairstyles, dressed in nicely tailored suits and seated beside women wearing stylish dresses and hairstyles over which some beautician labored the day before to get so straight. I also observe several women and men with their hair artfully arranged in braids, twists, and locks, as well as bouffant afros. As more people take their seats within the sanctuary, I see that many women are wearing West African–style head scarves and floor-length dresses and that the men have on dashikis and pantsuits made of kente cloth. Some women wearing boubous, the traditional gowns of West Africa, have permed hair, while others with natural hairstyles are clothed in Ann Taylor ensembles.

As I ponder this eclectic mesh of styles, a hush falls upon the gathering, and a young girl, the acolyte, enters the sanctuary to light the candle at the front of the church. She is followed by a distinguished-looking man with deep warm brown skin, low-cut graying black hair with a dramatic white patch in the front, and a most neatly trimmed salt-and-pepper mustache and beard. Wearing a black-and-white African pantsuit, this is Reverend Doctor Will Esuyemi Coleman, the resident theological scholar. He proceeds to the pulpit. As he does, the choir of some fifteen persons quietly take their places behind him. Simultaneously, eight women and men, each dressed in black, march with self-conscious authority up the aisle, splitting into two columns as they take their seats on the first row. These are the elders and deacons of the church. Until this point, other than the soft music of the jazz ensemble and the rustling of the persons entering the sanctuary, there has been a solemn hush. This is dramatically altered as the jazz drummers switch instruments to traditional drums and begin to play a loud and furious African rhythm.

And then enter eight dancing women. They have on varied African print fabrics knotted in intricate ways about their necks, shoulders, and hips. Each wears a different vibrant color, all are barefoot, and they swing their arms and lift their legs and twirl their bodies down the aisle to the beat of the drums in a well-choreographed ecclesiastical dance. The room pulsates with the music and the dancing, and the congregants keep time with the beat from their seats and watch the beautiful women. Even those, like myself, not used to boisterous dancing in the middle of a church aisle, could not help but to feel the spiritual energy infused into the rhythmic movement.

After several minutes, the dance comes to an end, the women elegantly march out, and the choir takes over. This time it is neither jazz nor traditional African drumming but a good old-fashioned gospel rendition of "Woke Up This Morning." Reverend Coleman's congregational prayer follows, and the program reads that Harambee is next. A honey-colored woman with thick brown locks atop her head takes the pulpit and explains that *Harambee* means "welcome" in Kiswahili. She asks the visitors to stand. Explaining that this is a different kind of church than they are probably used to, she directs their attention to the third page of the program, which reads as follows:

> We are an Afrocentric Christian ministry which utilizes the histories and cultures of African descended peoples as sources for biblical reflection and interpretation, ministry development and implementation, and evangelism in the community context where we exist. We believe that God is the Creator and sustainer of all things and people, and that God is sovereign. We believe, preach and teach that Jesus the Christ was a Northeast Afrikan Messiah of the Jewish faith who lived, died and was risen by the power of God, so that all who believe in God through him might be delivered from their sins and receive the gracious gift of eternal life.

Visitors are encouraged to consider making First Afrikan their new church home, and then the entire congregation is instructed to greet one another. What ensues is a friendly ten-minute melee as people move around the sanctuary hugging, greeting, and catching up on gossip. After a few unsuccessful attempts, Reverend Coleman is able to get everyone back into their seats, and the choir offers another musical selection, this time of the contemporary gospel variety. As they sing, I note that two more people have joined Reverend Coleman in the pulpit. One is a woman with penetrating brown eyes, regal locks, and a soft and sage-sounding voice. This is Elder "Mama" Itahari Toure and she is the director of education. The other person is about six feet tall, of deep brown skin with a dark beard and mustache and long brown locks that reach to his waist. A good-looking man, dressed in a brown, loose-fitting pantsuit with kente print on the pockets, this is Reverend Doctor Mark Ogunwale Keita Lomax, the pastor of First Afrikan Presbyterian Church. After the choir is finished, Reverend Lomax offers the pastoral prayer and then launches into his sermon with:

> There is a tendency to underestimate the life and the ministry of Jesus in North America. Week after week and sermon after sermon, we hear and see sweating radio and TV evangelists imaging Jesus as our personal Lord and Savior. More than that, and the thing that is so terribly disturbing to so many of us, is that the Jesus image is European. Jesus was not and could not have been in any sense European. He came from the wrong family to have been European. He came from the wrong part of the world to have been European. People say, Well it really doesn't matter. His ethnicity, his nationality, his color does not matter. Okay, fine. Let's tell the truth. If it doesn't matter, let's just tell the truth. And nothing but the truth. And ya'll know what that is. He came, he and his family, they resided there in ancient Kemet, many of us call it Egypt, which happens to be in Africa. And they were certainly African culturally. That is all they could have been.

Reverend Lomax continues to preach about Jesus and what African-descended Christian people should learn from his life. When the pastor has completed the sermon and as the musicians play softly behind him, he invites those who are so moved to join the congregation. The church begins to applaud as a young man wearing an Armani suit, his hair a low cap of dark curls, proceeds with a quiet resolve to where Reverend Lomax stands in the front of the sanctuary. The pastor takes him by the shoulder and asks if there are any others. Another round of clapping ensues as a woman with shoulder-length plaits and dressed in a simple black blouse and skirt walks up the aisle to join them. Reverend Lomax then bends his head in prayer over the two. In that prayer, he welcomes the newest members, and he prays for the congregation as a whole, as well as the entirety of the world.

After the prayer, the woman who earlier explained Harambee now takes charge of the newest converts, moving them off to the side. Reverend Lomax takes his seat, and Reverend Coleman rises to announce that it is Zawadi time. He explains that *Zawadi* means "gift" in Kiswahili, that this is now the time to give our offerings, and that we should follow the instructions of the ushers. As people prepare to make their offerings, Reverend Coleman reminds the congregation that it takes money to run a church and that before we give the contents of our wallets to Stonecrest, the local mall, that we should first generously give back a portion of what God has given to us. After a prayer of thanksgiving for the Zawadi, Reverend Coleman reads the announcements for the week and formally introduces the two newest members, Jeffrey Hamilton and Issa Fernbank.

Reverend Lomax returns to the pulpit to give the closing prayer. As he prays, the congregation moves in unison to bend their heads and extend their right hands in locked fists, that most striking symbol of black pride. I watch a small boy of three or four raise his left fist in emulation of the father who holds him, and I cannot help but to wonder what the child is learning in this space about what it means to be black, Afrocentric, and Christian. This book is a study of blackness within the context of an Afrocentric church.

Blackness

Blackness is lived in various ways. The experience of a working class Haitian American woman in Boston is different from the experience of an affluent man with brown skin in London, and both are different from that of a woman in Johannesburg whose light brown complexion signals her biracial heritage. The historical and contemporary racial politics of a nation, the intersections of race with gender, class, and ethnicity, the shade of brownness, and whether or not a person even identifies herself as black are just a few of the factors that shape the experience of the identity.

"Blackness" is a fluid concept in that it can refer to cultural and ethnic identity, sociopolitical status, an aesthetic and embodied way of being, a social and political consciousness, and a diasporic kinship. It is used as a description of skin color ranging from the palest cream to the richest chocolate. Blackness is a marker of enslavement, marginalization, criminality, filth, and evil. It is also a symbol of pride, beauty, elegance, strength, and depth. It is elusive and difficult to define and yet serves as one of the most potent and unifying domains of identity.

Blackness can be employed in multiple ways that may complement, contradict, and compete with one another. It is a foundation of social cohesion and allegiances and, at the same time, is a source of oppression and alienation. For some, blackness conflicts with other understandings of the self, such as class status, sexual orientation, and, for the multiracial, another racial identity. Cross-culturally, blackness is the foil to whiteness in terms of marking the boundaries of race, and, in both contentious and collaborative ways, all other racial identities are in conversation with or are negotiated in terms of blackness.

The complexity of blackness is evident in the national conversations concerning Barack Obama, the first black president of the United States. The son of an African father and a European American mother, Obama is challenged by those who question if he is in fact black or if his biracial heritage disqualifies him. Some challenge his credentials as African American as his African heritage is from the continent and not through domestic channels, while others decree that, by definition, one could not be more African American. In certain spheres his blackness inspires feelings of cultural kinship and political allegiance; in others, it is muted and made safe by his racial and cultural ties to whiteness; and, in yet others, it galvanizes fears of cultural threat and expressions of racist vitriol.

Then there are the ways in which the president's blackness intersects with his gender, class status, nationality, and ethnicity. How much anger can he express before triggering the dangerous black man stereotype, and how much deference can he show his wife before his very masculinity is questioned? As an affluent and Harvard-educated lawyer, can he identify with and defend the perspectives and needs of poor and working class African Americans, and does their shared blackness dictate that he do so? What of his relationship to Reverend Jeremiah Wright and the middle class church with a Black Nationalist sensibility that Obama and his family attended? Why would such a seemingly assimilated and accomplished middle class African American join a community critical of American racial and cultural politics? And of course, there are those who ask, "Is he American? Isn't he Muslim?"

These issues are not unlike those in circulation at First Afrikan Presbyterian Church. As an Afrocentric community, members wrestle with how to understand their blackness in relationship to Africa and in the context of U.S. racial politics. As a predominantly middle class congregation, they negotiate the boundaries of identification with both less-affluent African Americans and middle class European Americans. When the privileges of their bourgeoisie status collide with experiences of racism, members' conversations become rife with the tensions of double consciousness. A concept posited by W. E. B. DuBois, "double consciousness" describes the experiences of some African Americans as they wrestle with simultaneous feelings of assimilation into and alienation from the large national community. In addition, there are discourses within the church as to the ways in which ancestry, cultural practices, and political consciousness as well as exposure to whiteness and European culture shape the quality of a person's blackness. Black and womanist theologies are explored and critiqued as men and women navigate gender politics within the church and in their personal relationships. An Afrocentrically infused theology is also employed to develop a collective understanding of the racial and ethnic relationship between church members and people in the Bible.

First Afrikan Presbyterian Church is an established community whose Afrocentric ethos and religious format provide consistent access to discourses on how blackness is imagined and defined as well as examples of how blackness is performed and negotiated on both a collective and individual basis. Consequently, it is an ideal space in which to consider the myriad of questions blackness raises: Given the different experiences of blackness, its fluidity, and multiplicity, how does an individual or community understand and negotiate the identity? In what ways are people differently situated by the intersections of blackness with different axes of identity such as class and gender? What does blackness mean in an Afrocentric context, or in a theological context, or in a context that is neither? This book addresses these questions employing the perspectives and experiences of First Afrikan Presbyterian Church members.

Does the multivalence of blackness speak to its power as an identity, or to its murkiness as a concept, or to both? This book argues that the answer is both—blackness is simultaneously potent and ambiguous. In part, the power of race lies in its ability to address such ontological questions as, Where do I come from? or What are my cultural origins? Where do I belong? or Who are my people? and What is my purpose? or What should be the values and practices that shape my life? However, as race intersects with other axes of identity, such as class, gender, ethnicity, and nationality, the possible answers to these ontological questions begin to multiply, adopt varied nuances in different contexts and, at times, conflict with one another. As a consequence, the understanding of who one really is can become quite murky.

This book demonstrates that the middle class members of First Afrikan experience double consciousness or feelings of ambivalence as to where they belong and who they should be in terms of values and behaviors. I contend that the allure of Afrocentrism is that it is an established paradigm that advocates specific tenets for the origin, meaning, and practice of authentic blackness. Specifically, Afrocentrism maintains that because of its African genetic, spiritual, and cultural origins, blackness possesses an essential and immutable nature that transcends time, place, and all other axes of identity. Thus, through discourses of essentialism or ideas that there are natural and given ways to be black, an Afrocentric blackness is a powerful construction of the identity with the potential to resolve the double consciousness experienced by middle class African Americans.

Significantly, the class positionality and gender politics of the church's membership consistently destabilize essentialized constructions of blackness. For example, this book makes the case that because of the cultural capital and experiences of assimilation associated with their class status, First Afrikan's members understand themselves to have a blackness that is different from less-affluent African Americans. Furthermore, their middle class status allows the members to perform and rearrange the tenets of Afrocentrism in ways not as available to and with different consequences for working class and poor black Americans. In addition, womanist theology advocated by the leadership, embraced by some members, and wrestled with by others also results in competing versions of Afrocentrism and blackness. Consequently, within this one congregation are multiple and competing constructions of both blackness and Afrocentrism.

On the one hand, discourses of racial essentialism contribute to a powerful sense of shared identity; on the other hand, heterogeneous constructions of blackness simultaneously contribute to a sense of ambivalence. A core contention of this book is that this tension between essentialism and heterogeneity is not a problem to be solved; rather, it is a fundamental and necessary aspect of racial identity. Blackness is not one thing but a constellation of ideas, practices, values, meanings, histories, sociopolitical dynamics, and intersections with other axes of identity from which those so deemed as "black" strategically pick and choose in order to nurture community and navigate an individual sense of self. Furthermore, as an individual seeks to understand where she belongs and as a community negotiates what it values and will practice, the multiple elements of blackness are created, interpreted, rearranged, deconstructed, re-created, and reinterpreted.

Despite these convolutions, blackness is, in a sense, one thing: it is an essential cornerstone of racial ideology that provides a shared sense of identity that an individual may employ to determine who he is and who he should become. Although communities and individuals may have different constructions of and uses for this shared sense of identity, this book makes the case that the identity is most powerful during those moments when and in those spaces where people believe they are invested in, talking about, and practicing the same essential blackness.

This book describes how members use Afrocentrism to determine what authentic blackness is and how it should be practiced, how biblical narratives are employed to prove the value and essential nature of blackness, and how middle class status and womanist theology promote counternarratives of heterogeneity. Through an analysis of how First Afrikan Presbyterian Church negotiates the tensions between essentialist and heterogeneous constructions of blackness, this book provides a better understanding of the varied hues of blackness as well as the fundamental power of blackness as a shared identity.

An Afrocentric Church

As the project of Afrocentrism is to determine the authentic nature of blackness and how best to practice it, First Afrikan Presbyterian provides an especially distinctive lens through which to investigate the lived experience of blackness. In addition, the church context reveals how Afrocentrism is understood and practiced when married to Christian beliefs and narratives. The church also provides insight into why Afrocentrism retains ideological relevance and power in certain sectors of the African American community.

Proponents of Afrocentrism contend that many black people lack an authentic and healthy sense of self as they are ignorant of their African history and culture. For African Americans, this ignorance is a result of the transatlantic slave trade, which displaced them from their ancestral homes and disrupted their ties to the cultures of Africa. The ignorance is also the result, charge Afrocentric thinkers, of a deliberate distortion and, at times, erasure of Africa in the public imagination. Specifically, Afrocentric thought posits that Africa is misrepresented as a primitive place that has produced no meaningful thought or cultural accomplishment to compare with that achieved in Europe. Consequently, feelings of inferiority and inconsequence are inscribed into the psyches of African Americans as they are positioned as objects rather than agents of political, cultural, and intellectual change. Afrocentrism is understood as the corrective to Eurocentrism, the ethos considered responsible for both the deliberate distortion of African accomplishment and the feelings of inferiority among her descendants in the New World.

Eurocentric thought, or Eurocentrism, is the practice, conscious or otherwise, of centering and privileging European culture, values, and perspectives. As with any ethnocentric perspective, Eurocentrism judges other cultures by the values and standards of its own. Anthropologist Marimba Ani contends that it is not unusual or inherently wrong for a cultural group to privilege its worldview, whether Afrocentric or Eurocentric. However, she argues that European culture "is unique in its use of cultural thought in the assertion of political interest" and that the resultant cultural nationalism is oppressive to persons of color (1994: 567). In other words, European ethnocentrism married to European political might result in the oppression of others through political and cultural imperialism.

"Perhaps the most distinguishing character of Eurocentrism is its glamorization of its own historical heritage and experiences and its negation of the historicity of blacks, inducing the loss of a sense of history, cultural heritage and identity, rendering them vulnerable to Euro-American manipulation and domination" (Adeleke 1998: 2). Proponents of Afrocentrism contend that with an ethnocentric perspective privileging African culture, values, and perspectives, African-descended people become more substantively empowered social agents better motivated and able to improve their status within U.S. society.

Several criticisms have been leveled against Afrocentrism. A key critique is that scholars cherry-pick information or strategically emphasize and suppress certain aspects of African history and culture in the service of specific goals, such as the justification of antiwhite sentiment or the glorification of African civilization. Another complaint is that, as a deliberately ethnocentric paradigm, Afrocentrism simply reverses the direction of cultural bigotry it claims to oppose within Eurocentrism. Afrocentrists are accused of poor scholarship for emphasizing particular African cultural practices, such as the patriarchal family structure, and social achievements, such as Egyptian civilization, without attention to the myriad other African cultural practices and political organizations, such as female-headed households and rural villages. African-centered scholarship is also reproached for the tendency to privilege cultural practices and mores from the African past rather than those practiced within contemporary African societies.

However, as Wilson Moses has contended, Afrocentric people are not the only ones to commit the sin of selectively remembering and rearranging history: "The practice of creating a monumental past for one's race or nationality was hardly the invention of African vindicationists. Traditionally, fanciful Englishmen of letters who preferred not to think of their ancestry as crude barbarians could fancy themselves descendants of Trojan heroes" (1998: 11). Nor are Afrocentric scholars the only ones to have invented traditions from a pastiche of varied real and imagined cultural behaviors. For instance, many Scottish people believe that tartan plaids and bagpipes have great antiquity and are essential to their identity as Scottish. Trevor-Roper (1983) revealed, however, that these great traditions are in fact relatively recent and borrowed from the Highlanders, previously considered both barbaric and Irish. According to Hobsbawm (1983), cultural groups invent traditions and histories in order to meet crucial emotional needs and to fulfill significant ideological functions as they strive to understand themselves as a coherent group.

Gerald Early makes a similar argument in his discussion of the relationships between memory and identity. He posits that identity can be understood as constructed memory or, put another way, that the particular and idiosyncratic ways through which an individual categorizes, prioritizes, and edits past events provides the foundation for how that person understands herself. Moreover, the catalogue of personal memories is percolated through the collective memories of the group. So for Early, personal identity is "the psychological museum of the self that is so dependent on the idea of a collectivity, of a past derived from many" (1999: 703).

Furthermore, this museum of memories is constantly rearranged as individuals change their perspectives or interpretation of the evidence "in the never-ending need to reconstruct ourselves out of the remains of our ancestors, ourselves in another guise, so that they are both like us and unlike us" (Early 1999: 711). Within this logic, Afrocentrism can be understood as an evolving and fluid arrangement of collective history and knowledge with the objective of constructing an authentic and shared black self-consciousness.

In other words, while Afrocentrism may romanticize the cultural relationship between Africa and African America and selectively edit the history and contributions of African descended peoples, these dynamics are part of the process of creating a collective identity—a process that is fluid, evolving, and engaged in by all ethnic and cultural communities. The malleability of history and tradition is an artifact of a cultural group's efforts to understand who they are by creatively reconstructing who they were. Moreover, during this process, the factual truth is not necessarily required for a feeling of authenticity to be achieved.

Consequently, this book focuses on the resonance of Afrocentric beliefs within the members' constructions of black identity rather than judging the factualness of those beliefs. The concerns of Afrocentrism as an inherently flawed and problematic worldview or as a psychologically necessary and social empowering paradigm are not the focal point of this investigation. Both dwell too heavily in issues of accuracy rather than effect. Instead, this book makes its case for the richer examination of identity in this particular community with a focus on how members understand and practice Afrocentrism.

The significance of Afrocentrism and its influence upon a sense of blackness within the members' lives emerge when they speak of their reasons for joining First Afrikan. For instance, Jerome and Nina Kent are a young married couple in their late twenties with two children. Jerome has a perfectly coiffed beard and mustache, deep-set and thoughtful brown eyes, and thick rope-like locks neatly bundled into a ponytail. Nina is a light pecan brown with locks, pretty features, and a stunning white smile. Both are articulate, warm, and engaging. The couple explained that two years ago they attended a predominantly white Baptist church but never really felt a part of the congregation. A coworker suggested that Jerome look into First Afrikan. Jerome explains:

> So we went there one Sunday and we saw the African dancers coming down the aisle and we were like, whoa! And we were so, we just thought, that's it, you know. This is it—let's do this! And every time we went we felt the same. We went back three or four weeks after that and we joined after like the fourth week.

I interviewed another member, Valerie Owens, in her home shortly after she had returned from her nursing job. Forty-nine years of age, Valerie was raised in the Church of God in Christ and insisted that she "will always be COGIC to the core." Nevertheless, she joined First Afrikan Church with her husband:

> I was very impressed. And when I first came to First Afrikan, I enjoyed the lessons that Pastor Lomax was teaching. And I found it interesting because I grew up in the church and no other church that I had ever been in spoke about the Bible in terms of being a black person in America and being African at the same time. That was what really intrigued me.

The members of the church came from many different religious backgrounds, including Presbyterian as well as Baptist, Methodist, Episcopalian, Catholic, Nation of Islam, and Sunni Muslim. One woman previously practiced Buddhism while yet another had rejected organized religion altogether for most of her adulthood. Interestingly, nearly half of the members I interviewed did not consider themselves Presbyterian even after formally joining the congregation, and at least one person told me that he did not really consider First Afrikan a church but rather an Afrocentric learning center. For most, whether considering themselves Presbyterian or not, First Afrikan was a place where an Afrocentric ideology could be married to a Christian theology.

Members frequently emphasized that the presentation of the Bible as an African text and of biblical characters as black helped them to more fully embrace Christianity. They spoke of how pictures of a blond Jesus and media representations of the biblical characters as European had been alienating for them and that it was such a relief to be given evidence that this was not in fact the case. Several of the women were to tell me how upon the first Sunday of attendance, "it just felt right and I cried." The members with whom I spoke believe that Eurocentrism deliberately distorts the historical achievement and cultural contributions of Africa, thus undermining the psychological health and cultural resilience of African Americans. They have faith that learning, celebrating, and practicing African-centered ways of being and doing will result in a more psychologically, socially, and politically empowered community. They also believe that an African-centered theology is the most spiritually fulfilling way for a person of African descent to be in relationship with God.

I asked Reverend Lomax what he thought motivated people to join the church. He responded:

> You know, I don't really know. I'd like to think that I was just a great and brilliant preacher. [*He laughs.*] I think for some people its Malcolm-esque. It's that hard, rhetorical diatribe against everything that is wrong with black folks. For other people, I think it is the integration of Afrocentric philosophy. It helps people to see how the story of scripture is an African story and connects to our story as African Americans. Some people, I think it is entertainment.

Elder "Mama" Itahari Toure was of the opinion that people attended the church because it was a space in which they could voice their frustration with and pain from the racism encountered in their daily lives:

> People are here for the same reason our people gravitated to the nation of Islam, the same reason our people gravitated to Marcus Garvey, the same reason people have gravitated to anyone who was courageous enough to say everything is not alright with us and it's not okay that it's not alright. So I think that's the main reason—because you're giving voice to my reality. And even though I might not have the courage to change my reality, the fact that somebody somewhere is giving voice is a flame I want to be next to. So for an hour and a half, I feel okay that I'm upset about this, I feel angry about this, and it's okay, and so all my emotions I can bring forth.

That First Afrikan services should provide a release valve for pain and anger related to racial oppression seems correct. During services, one could not help but note the nodding heads as Reverend Coleman prayed for heavenly intervention on behalf of those dealing with personal experiences of struggle and injustice. One is also struck by the shouts of "tell the truth" as Reverend Lomax castigated the Bush administration or the gales of laughter signaling agreement as he lambasted some happening in the news he considered especially Eurocentric. Sitting in a pew among the congregants, I could plainly see the enjoyment of the polemical and often poetic way that the pastor took to task those who slighted the black community.

Of course, political critique and social protest have been elements of black congregations since slavery. Through religion, African Americans have historically found "voice, indeed multiple and variegated voices, to speak not only of their spiritual quest and fulfillment but of their earthly trials and social yearnings as well" (Baer and Singer 2002: xvii). From clandestine worship among enslaved Africans, to the post-Emancipation independent church movement, and, notably, to the activism of churches during the Civil Rights era, the Black Church has functioned as a site from which to articulate social frustration, to mobilize political action, and to build community (Baer and Singer 2002; Raboteau

2001). In that sense, First Afrikan is engaging in a long-standing African American theological tradition.

Religiously Communal

The marriage of Afrocentrism and the Black Church is an especially interesting one as religion and African-centered thought share many of the same characteristics and serve similar social functions. From an anthropological perspective, the functions of religion include, but are not limited to addressing the meaning of life with explanations for how humans came to be, our purpose while living, and our fate after death; providing codes for how to properly live and rituals to reinforce those principles; and offering reasons for suffering as well as mechanisms to navigate hardships and uncertainty. These shared insights into suffering, morality, and meaning foster solidarity and an intense sense of community. Consequently, religion has three fundamental characteristics: an ideology, a set of rituals, and a communal sensibility. Similarly, Afrocentrism has an ideology and set of rituals that are employed to maintain and sustain community among those of African descent.

Ideology

An ideology is a worldview or a shared set of beliefs, values, and attitudes. The ideological tenets of most religions are conveyed, in part, through narratives or myths that explain the origin of humanity, the purpose of life, and the process of death. Religious myths recount the experiences, thoughts, and actions of select prophets and heroes and thereby provide believers with an ordained set of truths, values, and behaviors. Through these narratives, the religion's ideology "poses a set of dilemmas, provides the answers to those questions, and simultaneously constructs an interpretive narrative of the world and of the group" (Harris-Lacewell 2004: 17).

Afrocentrism is also a worldview that provides adherents with explanations for the origin and meaning of blackness, a shared interpretation of their racial and ethnic experiences, and a set of directions for living an authentic and meaningful African-centered life. For example, at First Afrikan, the Sunday sermons and Wednesday night Bible study classes, with their emphasis upon the Bible as an African text and Jesus as a black man, furnish members with not only a vision of their spiritual destiny but also their ethnic and racial destinies. The efforts of members to wear African clothing and to learn Kiswahili words are a few of the rituals by which fellow African-centered people recognize one another, while the Afrocentric theology and political critiques are strategies by which the community navigates racial oppression. Finally, the discourses within the church concerning the blessings and perils of the intersections of blackness, middle class status, and gender are the narratives through which members learn the prescribed values and behaviors of a spiritually and racially healthy African American. In these ways, the Afrocentric Christianity of the church "provides individuals with a sense of the value and meaning of their lives" by revealing "profound truths and guidance for action in the world" (Warms 2009: 387).

Ritual

A ritual is a social act that signals acceptance of a common social and moral order. In "religious ritual, people attempt to forge a link between themselves and gods, ancestors, enlightenment and the good of the world as they understand it" and therefore, through ritual, a person's understanding and behavior are affected and possibly changed (Warms 2009: xiii). Rituals can be especially important to those groups that consider themselves under cultural assault and employ religion as a resistance strategy to the loss of cultural integrity. Such religious efforts are anthropologically understood as revitalization movements or organized efforts to eliminate alien values and behaviors while reinvigorating traditional customs connected to previous generations. Revitalization movements employ ritual to reteach the authentic culture and thus transform a group member corrupted by the alien customs into a true believer and practitioner.

At First Afrikan Church, there are various sets of rituals intended to connect members to the ancestors and an enlightened sense of cultural identity. Furthermore, Afrocentrism is a revitalization movement, as First Afrikan employs ritual to eliminate alien values through the conversion of problematically Eurocentric black people into authentically Afrocentric black people. Put another way, "One is both born Black and becomes Black. Just as Christians undergo baptism to demonstrate their membership in their faith-based community, Afrocentric true believers are expected to undergo similar conversion rituals" (Collins 2006: 90). For example, at First Afrikan Church, a convert to Afrocentrism often publicly declares that her consciousness and behavior have been fundamentally altered through social acts such as adopting an African name, changing her style of dress and hairstyle to those considered more authentically African, and by making pilgrimages to African countries.

Chapter 2, "Situating the Self: Becoming Afrikan in America," describes the conversion rituals of First Afrikan members. It elucidates the ways in which these rituals are engaged to signal membership to outsiders, to nurture the bonds between those in the community, and to remind the convert of her more authentically African blackness. Importantly, the same act of Afrocentric blackness may be interpreted differently by observers and among practitioners. Thus, a consideration of these rituals provides insight into how Afrocentrism is performed and demonstrates the varied meanings of blackness embedded within those performances.

Community

Anthropologist Victor Turner put forth that the conversion ritual is experienced in three phases. In the first phase, the individual becomes separated from one understanding of the self, such as a Eurocentrically coded black identity, then passes into a liminal phase of being neither completely the old identity nor the new identity, and finally, the person fully incorporates the new understanding of self, such as an Afrocentrically coded black identity.

When this experience of conversion happens on a collective level, it results in communitas, or an intense community spirit of solidarity and togetherness. "It is not effortless companionship that can arise between friends, coworkers, or professional coworkers any day" but, rather, "a transformative experience that goes to the root of each person's being and finds in that root something profoundly communal and shared" (Turner 1969: 138).

Mutual definitions of identity, a collective worldview, and shared experiences foster this deep spirit of community, just as competing definitions and worldviews can complicate and even erode feelings of communitas. This book examines the ways in which First Afrikan's construction of community is influenced by shared understandings of blackness, and it probes the means through which individuals negotiate the tensions created by competing constructions of the identity.

Communitas and Blackness

A communal sensibility may be cultivated through a collective narrative that explains shared experiences of suffering and provides the means by which to navigate the distress. For example, black liberation theology situates racial oppression within the context of divine politics and advocates the end of oppression for peoples of African descent. During slavery, African Americans celebrated Moses and his deliverance of the Israelites from Egyptian slavery. In contemporary liberation theology, Jesus is understood as the champion of the oppressed, and his teachings are used to critique acts of social, economic, and political injustice.

In addition to a perspective on oppression, black liberation theology also offers a counterdiscourse to Eurocentric narratives within both Christian hermeneutics and American cultural politics. At First Afrikan Church, Jesus and African Americans share blackness and experiences of being misunderstood and unjustly persecuted by the society. Communitas is fostered through this Christian Afrocentric counterdiscourse as church members have the opportunity to exchange interpretations of the truth, to link their individual experiences to group narratives, and to devise strategies for addressing group problems (Harris-Lacewell 2004). Significantly, the sense of community depends, in part, upon an essentialized construction of blackness.

Essentialism posits that blackness is a quality that naturally inheres in persons of African descent regardless of time and place. Within Afrocentric theology, this blackness is shared by both biblical characters and contemporary African Americans, thus undergirding a sense of kinship in terms of shared consciousness and behavior, a sense of solidarity in terms of shared experiences of oppression, and a sense of collective destiny in terms of both spiritual and cultural politics. A powerful catalyst of communitas, essentialism has powerful consequences.

One consequence is that group members come to believe that there are authentic and appropriate ways to be black as well as inauthentic and erroneous ways to be black. Shared articles of faith and rituals to identify authentically black members are developed by privileging certain markers of racial and ethnic similarity while repressing markers of difference within the group. In other words, among the varied manifestations of blackness, only one is considered authentic, and the others are viewed with suspicion and, at times, rejected.

At First Afrikan Church, discourses of essentialized blackness are especially prominent when congregants engage in theological discussions but are muted when congregants engage in discussions of their blackness outside of theological contexts. In the latter case, discourses tend to construct blackness as inherently heterogeneous or that it is diverse in content and can be performed in various ways. For example, during Bible study, Jesus and Afrocentric peoples share the same authentic blackness while others possess a lesser blackness. However, when comparing their middle class values, tastes, and behaviors to those of working class and poor black Americans, members allow that there is not one authentic blackness but multiple blacknesses, and they resist, though do not completely negate, the idea that one is lesser than the other.

Chapter 3, "'Who I Am and Whose I Am': Race and Religion," first explores how, through interpretations of the Bible as an African text and imaginings of biblical characters as black people, Afrocentric ideology provides explanations for racial oppression and principles for a spiritually and culturally healthy African-centered life. The chapter then analyzes the ways that blackness is defined in both theological and secular contexts. Through a consideration of these competing constructions of blackness, the chapter demonstrates that the nature of blackness is inherently and simultaneously essentialist and heterogeneous.

Liminality and Incorporation

During religious conversion, liminality is understood as that space where a person is betwixt and between who he was before experiencing this change in spiritual consciousness and who he will be after fully incorporating the change. Members of First Afrikan Church likely experience feelings of liminality as they are transitioning from Eurocentric ways of thinking and being to Afrocentric ways. However, Chapter 4 focuses on a sense of perpetual liminality in which the person does not attempt to transition from one identity to another but rather endeavors to stand at the threshold of two identities simultaneously. The chapter explores how, for the middle class African American, this positionality is often experienced as being neither fully incorporated into blackness nor fully incorporated into middle class status.

Another way of understanding this experience is double consciousness, or the conundrum posed when a person holds two or more constructions of identity that in some measure conflict with one another. On the one hand, for the middle class black person, there is the contention that achieving middle class status is a positive thing in that it reflects worthiness and the ability to overcome racist oppression. On the other hand, there is the concern that upward mobility may create alienation from poorer blacks and the fear that blackness may be corrupted by overidentifying with the white middle class. Taken together, these arguments suggest that the black middle class person may feel both allegiance to and alienation from the racial identity he shares with poorer black people as well as the class identity he shares with middle class white people. He is simultaneously of two minds—a double conscience.

The fourth chapter, "Ebony Affluence: Afrocentric Middle Classness," considers how Afrocentrism is a key component, used in multiple ways, as members negotiate the sustained liminality of being both black and middle class. It also considers how double consciousness concerning class and blackness influences the relationship between blackness and national identity. Consequently, the chapter provides perspective as to how individuals negotiate the tensions between blackness and another axis of identity.

Whereas the friction between blackness and middle class status is experienced as perpetual liminality, for other competing conceptualizations of identity, there is the possibility for full incorporation into both. The fifth chapter, "Eve's Positionality: Afrocentric and Womanist Ideologies," analyzes the dynamics between the seemingly competing and antagonistic counterdiscourses within the church. Womanist theology serves as a counterdiscourse to black liberation theologies that do not attend to the particular ways in which women are oppressed and to feminist theologies that ignore acts of racial injustice encountered by women of color. Afrocentric ideology is a counterdiscourse to Eurocentric thought. However, in certain manifestations, Afrocentrism relies heavily upon patriarchal readings of the Bible and sexist approaches to black cultural politics. The leadership of First Afrikan Church is gradually introducing womanist theology as a counterdiscourse to those dynamics of female marginalization and oppression.

The chapter examines Afrocentric and womanist ideologies' places of intersection, agreement, and contradiction in terms of gendered biblical interpretations as well as the expectations of gender behavior within the lives of the members. Through a consideration of how much Afrocentric ideology and womanist theology do and do not in fact conflict within the belief systems of the congregation, the chapter also measures the possibility of church members incorporating both perspectives. In so doing, the chapter provides an example of the negotiation of and possible reconciliation between competing conceptualizations of black identity.

Conclusion

Through an analysis of their own words on the topics of blackness, middle class status, and gender politics, this book provides insight into how a community of contemporary African Americans understands themselves. Furthermore, it moves beyond theoretical discussions of the intersections of race, class, and gender by providing an ethnographic analysis of the lived experience of these identities in the context of an Afrocentric religious community. Finally, it considers the ways in which blackness is performed, defined, and negotiated with attention to the dynamics inherent within blackness, essentialism, and heterogeneity; the tension between blackness and another axis of identity, middle class status; and the relationship between two conceptualizations of blackness, Afrocentric ideology and womanist theology.

Although this volume focuses on discourses of race, class, and gender, First Afrikan is foremost a Christian church whose most consistent messages are that of love toward others and an enduring relationship with God. This theological concern permeates this book because it would be disrespectful toward the people who so graciously invited me into their sacred space to allow that aspect of how they understand themselves to get lost in my analysis. The next chapter, "The First Afrikan Way: Method and Context," provides context for understanding First Afrikan Presbyterian Church by describing the evolution of African-centered ideology within the Presbyterian congregation as well as the church's similarities and differences in comparison to other Afrocentric religious communities. It also describes the methodology used to conduct this study.

1

The First Afrikan Way

Method and Context

The History and Hope of Afrocentrism

The term "Afrocentrism" was coined by the academic Molefi Kete Asante, who defines it as a "frame of reference wherein phenomena are viewed from the perspective of the African person. The Afrocentric approach seeks in every situation the appropriate centrality of the African person" (1991: 171). Afrocentric scholars of history, literature, sociology, psychology, and other disciplines have attempted to make African intellectual inquiry the center of understanding for persons of African descent.

Although strongly associated with Asante, Afrocentrism has deeper roots than his articulation, as it extends back to nineteenth-century African American intellectuals such as Martin R. Delany, Carter G. Woodson, and W. E. B. DuBois. In their work, these scholars investigated the achievements of various African cultures and sought to demonstrate what African descended peoples had contributed to human civilization. Delany, for instance, wrote, *Principia of Ethnology: The Origin of Race and Color, with an Archeological Compendium of Ethiopian and Egyptian Civilization* (1880), a comparative study of Africa and Europe in which he extolled the preeminence of Africa by citing its wealth and the antiquity of its civilization. Among Woodson's prolific writings are *African Heroes and Heroines* and *The African Background Outlined*. For his part, DuBois focused not only upon the history of Africa when editing the *Crisis* newspaper and *The Encyclopedia Africana* but also upon the idea of an essentially African identity shared by all throughout the Diaspora. In *The Souls of Black Folk*, his notions of race, soul, and consciousness were borrowed from African metaphysics and, furthermore, were employed to argue for an African way of being based upon history and culture that inhered in persons of African descent (Rath 1997).

Although they wrote a considerable time before the term "Afrocentrism" was coined, these early scholars are considered proponents of Afrocentric thought as they labored toward the goals of the depiction of Africans as historical actors, the rehabilitation of the historical and cultural heritage of those of African descent, and the recognition of Africa as the foundation of knowledge about black peoples (Adeleke 2001). The works of intellectuals such as Delany, Woodson, DuBois, and many others "assumed a rehabiliatory, redemptionist and contributionist character" as they represented "Blacks as positive historical actors, people with a rich heritage of history and culture" (Adeleke 2001: 23).

Borrowing not only from these American intellectuals, Asante's work is also built upon the scholarship of Senegalese theorist Cheikh Anta Diop. Diop's key premise is that ancient Egyptians created the foundations of both African and European civilization through the contribution of significant aspects of astronomy, geometry, law, architecture, art, mathematics, medicine, and philosophy. A particular thorn in Diop's side was the contention that Egypt was not in fact African, despite its obvious geographic location; his research "supports the idea of a White conspiracy of history to discredit or ignore Black civilization and advocates the need for proper knowledge of an African past in order to unify Blacks beyond simply the idea that they share a common oppression" (Early 1999: 709).

The recovery projects of these nineteenth-century scholars, as well as those of more contemporary scholars—including Asante, George G. M. James, Asa Hilliard, and Martin Bernal—assert that, in order to be a mentally and spiritually healthy person of African descent, one must know and privilege his or her Africanness above all else. Moreover, the

Afrocentric paradigm considers it a political imperative that African-descended people articulate their own culturally specific perspectives about society: "By believing that our way of viewing the universe is just as valid as any, we will achieve the kind of transformation that we need to participate fully in a multicultural society. However, without this kind of centeredness, we bring almost nothing but a darker version of whiteness" (Asante 1998: 8). Therefore, Afrocentrism can be understood as an attempt on the part of African-descended peoples to redefine themselves as subjects rather than objects of history and to view the world from a perspective that is grounded in blackness (Cobb 1997).

Although a number of African Americans, including scholars, clergy, and political leaders, have privileged African history and culture in constructions of identity and community since the time of slavery, it was not until the 1980s and 1990s that African-centered thinking became a cultural movement. African Americans throughout the country adapted school curriculum, worship services, dress, hairstyles, naming practices, and other key facets of everyday life to reflect and celebrate African heritage. Proponents of Afrocentrism encouraged African Americans to reconnect with their African roots and exhorted the larger society to acknowledge the contributions of African peoples to the world and American society.

Significantly, the 1980s and 1990s also marked the presidencies of Ronald Reagan and George H. W. Bush and their conservative agendas, which opposed significant portions of the Civil Rights and Voting Rights Acts, as well as many affirmative action policies. In addition, during the decade there were increasing rates of drug use, imprisonment, and poverty within many black communities. A major racialized event during this period was the Rodney King incident. In 1991, Rodney King, an African American man, was severely beaten by white police officers who were acquitted despite the incident having been videotaped. This outcome resulted in several race riots throughout black communities. It could be argued that, frustrated by the loss of progress since the Civil Rights movement, African Americans embraced Afrocentrism as a way to counter these sobering dynamics.

Afrocentrism posits that while white racism is responsible for many of the oppressive aspects of black life, its most deleterious impact is upon the self-esteem and cultural pride of African-descended people.

Asante and other advocates of Afrocentrism put forth that, if black people had a better understanding of their history, traditions, and values as a people, they would be better equipped to counter the effects of racism. For example, they suggest that Afrocentric schools could provide children with pride in their African heritage, positive black role models, and a supportive environment that expected them to succeed. They argue that the public school system has provided few of these factors and that without them, black children, particularly boys, are more prone to do poorly in school, drop out, become teenaged parents, and participate in the drug trade.

In his critique of Afrocentrism, Algernon Austin contends that this perspective reflects cultural conservatism and middle class bias within African America. He writes, "Afrocentrism tends to the conservative position which attacks social problems by changing values, as opposed to the liberal position which attacks social problems by equalizing resources" (2006: 146). His argument is that Afrocentrism perceives black culture as the main problem rather than identifying the lack of resources and the barriers of institutional racism as the more crucial issues. More specifically, advocates believe that an African-centered ideology and lifeway could make black culture healthier by improving self-esteem and inculcating better family values among poorer African Americans. Austin sees this contention as the continuation of the project of the black middle class to uplift the black poor and a version of the American middle class immigrant success story: "Just as middle-class whites talk about how the cultural values of their immigrant ancestors pulled the family up from poverty, Afrocentrism can be seen as attempting to create the same ethnic success by following the same logic" (2006: 168). In this scenario, female-headed households, drug use, low educational outcomes, the dearth of black businesses, and increasing violence within poorer African American communities could be counteracted if black people retained and practiced their African cultural values in much the same way as Irish, Asian, and Jewish immigrants had.

While this Afrocentrist perspective ignores the disparate impacts of voluntary versus involuntary immigration, the assimilationist trajectories of all American immigrant groups, the historical legacy of differential access to social mobility based on skin color, and the problem of blaming the victim and his culture, it nevertheless had resonance within the black community. To different degrees, many did indeed embrace Afrocentrism as an avenue to empower and improve the black community. An increasing number of parents gave their children African or Muslim names, enrolled them in Afrocentric schools, and celebrated Kwanzaa as a family. I was in college in Atlanta during the early 1990s and clearly remember the popularity of Afrocentric iconography and rhetoric. Throughout the city were several Afrocentric bookstores, food venues, clothing stores, hair salons, and cultural centers. In certain areas of the city, one could feel quite conspicuous without a natural hairstyle or African-inspired piece of jewelry or clothing. It was during this period in the early 1990s that Reverend Lomax established First Afrikan Presbyterian.

An Experiment in Progress

First Afrikan was originally named Salem Presbyterian Church. Established in 1893 as a predominantly white congregation, Salem Presbyterian elected to dissolve the congregation in 1991 as the changing racial demographics of the area made it difficult to hold the church together or to retain pastoral leadership. In 1993, efforts were made to resuscitate the church, and Reverend Mark Lomax was appointed to the "New" Salem Presbyterian Church to serve the now predominantly African American congregation. By the end of the year, one hundred and fifty persons were interested in becoming members, and a decision was made to rename the church First Afrikan Presbyterian. As a cultural and political statement, the church's name was spelled with a *k* as *c* is not a letter/sound found in most indigenous African languages.

Why did the church decide to become an Afrocentric congregation? The official history is that a steering committee of twelve people in cooperation with Reverend Lomax worked together to develop a mission and vision statement for the congregation. During discussions and debates, which took place over the course of several weeks, the idea of an Afrocentric-based theology was embraced by the majority. When I asked persons who were part of the founding congregation about the move toward Afrocentrism, it was reiterated that the decision was a collaborative effort between the membership and leadership. I posit that additional pivotal factors were the popularity of Afrocentrism in

Atlanta during the early 1990s as well as the personal Afrocentric ideology of Reverend Lomax.

At the time of his appointment, Reverend Lomax was completing his doctorate at Union Theological Seminary in Ohio and decided to write his dissertation on the efficacy of a lectionary that sought to teach Afrocentric Christian consciousness. Completed in 1995, the dissertation, "The Effects of an Afrocentric Hermeneutic in a Developing Congregation," included a thesis that stated that "an Afrocentric world view can liberate and empower African American Christians to love themselves more dearly, determine for themselves their God-given purpose for being in the world, and empower them to become active agents in the process of forming liberated and empowered families, churches and communities" (Lomax 1995:1). He chose First Afrikan to test his hypothesis.

Although Reverend Lomax was quite clear about and determined in his mission for the congregation, he encountered resistance. For example, just as the new congregation was attaining a measure of membership and fiscal stability, one of the more powerful female members lobbied to move away from the Afrocentric theology. Reverend Lomax recounts that "one of the elders who had a lot of power, not just formal power as an elder, but informal power as well, in terms of relationships and all, felt that we ought to switch back to a more Eurocentric presentation now that we had gotten the church to a certain point." That point was having grown from 68 members to nearly 250 within the span of a few months. I asked Lomax how this elder expressed what he called a "Eurocentric presentation," and he explained that she wanted to more fully employ the Presbyterian hymnal, to talk more about John Calvin, and to emphasize the Presbyterian polity. An argument ensued between the two, culminating in a claim by the elder, who was a lawyer, that the church was operating outside of the constitutional boundaries of the Presbyterian Church and that all members were now legally liable. This injected fear into the congregation, and the attendance dropped from 240 to 124. This woman was to eventually leave the congregation.

Later a contingent of professional women from the women's ministry led a revolt in the opposite direction by arguing that the church should not be Christian at all but rather practice traditional African religions. Dialogue about this continued for six or seven weeks. At one point, according to Lomax, he asked, "Which one of you will sacrifice the first goat? Because when you talk about traditional African religion, you are talking about animal sacrifice. I don't do that. I am a Christian pastor. So, which one of you will take the responsibility of preparing the sacrifice?" The women were not amused by his comments. Nor were they soothed by his articles for the church newsletter, *Talking Drum*, in which he talked about the definition of Afrocentric Christian ministry and the origins of Christianity in Africa. Things came to a head one Sunday in 1995, when the ministers processed into the sanctuary wearing blue Geneva gowns, a style of clerical vestments with wide sleeves first worn in Europe. "This group of sisters who were sitting together, got up and turned their backs in protest over the fact that we were wearing Eurocentric garb. Which was a powerful thing. It was very powerful. We talked about it, but the sisters and their husbands and children all left."

According to Reverend Lomax, trying to find a workable middle ground between these two poles represented by the different camps within the church has necessitated caution and some experimentation. During its twelve-year existence, the demography of the First Afrikan community has been in rather consistent flux, as its ranks have swollen and shrunk. Reverend Lomax reflected that the current congregation is probably the fifth or sixth for the church, as people have come and gone, some for the usual reasons people join and leave congregations and others for reasons particular to the Afrocentric theology of this church. This book focuses on the membership of the church between October 2003 and August 2005 and on the content of the Afrocentric Christian theology offered by the leadership during this period.

Somewhat Native Anthropology

In October 2003, I met with the Reverend Lomax, explained my project to him, and asked permission to use the church as my study site. As part of my research, I conducted participant observation during Sunday morning services, Wednesday night Bible study classes, new member orientation classes, vacation Bible school, and other church events. When attending classes and other smaller church gatherings, I explained my project and asked the permission of participants to include the session in my research.

In addition, I conducted semiformal interviews with thirty members of the congregation and with the three senior members of the church leadership. I met with individuals in the classrooms of the church after service, at their homes after work, or at restaurants when we were both hungry. Each person with whom I conducted an interview was given a verbal explanation of my project and asked to sign a consent form that explained his or her rights as a subject in my study. Participants were asked both verbally and in the body of the consent form for permission to tape-record them.

It is important to note that, while I do use the real names of Reverend Lomax, Reverend Coleman and Elder Toure, with their permission, all other names of First Afrikan members are pseudonyms. In order to protect the anonymity of the church members, I have altered identifying details in my descriptions of their physical appearances, occupations, and locations.

As I am an African American woman, this project can be considered native anthropology. A native anthropologist studies her own community. In many ways, my blackness helped me to gain entrée and establish rapport within the church community. For one thing, I easily blended into the congregation with no one questioning my presence at services, Bible studies, or participation in conversations. For another, members often assumed that my presence in the church indicated that I either accepted or was open to Afrocentric theology. In fact, during many of my interviews, participants inquired how long I had been a member of the church, and I had to remind them that I was not a member but a visiting anthropologist.

This smooth transition raised concern about that special pitfall of native anthropology—one is so integrated into the community that significant moments are ignored because they seem natural and given. I grew up in Mississippi, and both of my parents are United Methodist pastors. Therefore, to be sure, despite my best efforts, I probably overlooked important dynamics that another not so familiar with the Southern black church would have not. And yet, the context was not so familiar to me because of its most distinguishing feature—Afrocentrism. I do not consider myself to be Afrocentric and, until my sojourn at the church, had only a rudimentary understanding gleaned sporadically from Afrocentric acquaintances and academic critiques.

The African drumming and dancing, the use of the African language Kiswahili, the donning of African clothing, and the consistent rhetoric concerning Africanness in a church setting created a somewhat foreign environment for me. Consequently, there were key moments during my research when I was not a native anthropologist and required guidance in order to navigate this particular cultural context. Luckily, the church leadership had developed several strategies to teach Afrocentric ideology and theology to a novice such as myself.

An Afrocentric Curriculum

During my time at the church, Reverend Mark Lomax, Reverend Will Coleman, and Elder Itahari Toure provided the core spiritual leadership and African-centered teaching of the church. Reverend Lomax, the pastor, received a Doctor of Ministry degree from United Theological Seminary in Dayton, Ohio, and served as the pastor of churches in North Carolina and Atlanta before coming to First Afrikan. In addition, he teaches at the Interdenominational Theological Center, a seminary in Atlanta, and his areas of specialty include African traditional religions and African American religious history. Reverend Coleman, the resident theological scholar, received his Ph.D. from Graduate Theological Union Seminary in Berkeley, California. Also a professor at the Interdenominational Theological Center, he specializes in the philosophy of religion, interpretation theory, and biblical spirituality. Elder Toure is the director of education and was completing her doctorate of theology during my time at the church. She describes her work at First Afrikan as an extension of her life, as she has identified as Afrocentric since the 1970s, has considerable experience with grassroots organizations, and was instrumental in founding three independent schools.

This well-educated leadership triumvirate strives to create an environment in which education is deeply valued. During sermons or Bible study classes, each is comfortable employing esoteric vocabulary and hermeneutic references. They frequently emphasize the academic basis for both their biblical and Afrocentric knowledge, and, on church documents, Lomax's and Coleman's names are often accompanied by both the "Rev." and "Dr." prefixes. The members, too, make reference to their spiritual and African-centered scholarship and are not shy to note their other academic achievements. This is a well-educated church and proud of it.

And yet the church does not have an air of academic elitism. Lomax, Coleman, and Toure are also just as likely to pepper their teaching with black vernacular and to employ the poetic and kinetic style associated with African American preaching. Knowledge gained from more organic sources, such as kinfolk and local communities, is just as valued as that from the ivory towers. Frequent yet smooth are the shifts from academic discourse to folk discourse by the leadership of the church. At key moments, each minister strategically uses academic speech to mark the middle class identity of the church and to validate the often marginalized African-centered perspectives discussed there. Black folk speech is employed just as strategically to reinforce notions of shared cultural experiences and knowledge as well as racial pride. This is the tenor of Sunday sermons and its Afrocentric pedagogy.

An important component of First Afrikan's ministry is its Center for Afrikan Biblical Studies. The mission of the center is to "cultivate and promote communal and personal reflective journeys using Afrikan spiritual principles to deepen and enrich being and service" (www. firstafrikanchurch.org). As is predictable, considering the background of the leadership and as is usual in Presbyterian churches, much of the church programming has a collegiate format. Each year, First Afrikan chooses a core topic, and during the fall, spring, and summer semesters, various classes are offered during Wednesday night Bible study to the membership. Although free, one is required to register for a class, attendance is taken, textbooks are required, and homework is assigned, including participation in online chatrooms. Although no grades are given, several courses do have a prerequisite class.

The Wednesday night Bible study classes are organized to reach people at different levels of expertise and with different agendas. For example, there is a Bible study series that takes members through both a traditional and Afrocentric reading of each book of the Bible. Spirituality courses consider the varied religious traditions of African people throughout the Diaspora, with Christianity being only one of those considered. Also included in the curriculum are classes that are not necessarily theological but attend to African history and culture as well as African identity.

In addition to the Wednesday night Bible studies, there is lay leader programming that includes a guest lecturer series, guided conversation exercises, journaling, and weekend retreats. During the summer, instead of weekly Bible study classes there is vacation Bible school, Camp Taifa, during which members meet each night for two weeks for an in-depth study of a selected topic. Finally, periodically during the year, special topic classes are offered on financial stability, child rearing, or negotiating romantic relationships. For any class offered, there is usually an accompanying packet that explains the organization of the course, suggests writing or discussion exercises, provides literature on the topic, and recommends literature for further reading.

The leadership of First Afrikan considers the church a space in which to learn about and celebrate African heritage and culture and to spiritually evolve with an appreciation of the connections between Africanness and Christianity. Each minister feels called to nurture both a Christian spirituality and an Afrocentric consciousness among the congregants. A diverse congregation of some seven hundred members has responded to this call.

Afrocentric Congregations

First Afrikan is one of several congregations in the United States to interweave Afrocentric ideology into its theology. In Atlanta, there are at least two other Afrocentric churches, the Shrine of the Black Madonna and the African Hebrew Israelites. The Shrine of the Black Madonna is a Pan-African Orthodox Christian Church emphasizing Black Nationalism with other congregations in Detroit, Houston, and Calhoun Falls, South Carolina. Jaramogi Abebe Agyeman, born Albert B. Cleage, founded the Pan-African Orthodox Christian Church in 1975 with the theological mandate to free people of African descent within the United States from all forms of oppression, especially the myth of black inferiority. Consequently, Jesus is called the Black Messiah, Mary is referred to as the Black Madonna, and the biblical Hebrew nation is considered a black one. The church combines Catholic and African religious traditions and teaches members the art of Pa-Kua, which includes meditation, yoga, and tai chi with the intent of psychologically, physically, and spiritually healing the trauma of racial oppression. The church in Atlanta provides several services to the community, including direct aid, legal and medical referrals, computer skills training, and tutoring. It has a book store, cultural center, and communal land farm project that is quite respected by many members of the larger community.

Somewhat more controversial are the African Hebrew Israelites, with congregations in Atlanta, Chicago, and Israel. They consider themselves to be descendants of the Ten Lost Tribes and put forth that, after being expelled from Jerusalem, their ancestors migrated to West Africa and were eventually enslaved and transported to the United States. The founder of the spiritual group, Ben Ammi, born Ben Carter, attests that the Archangel Gabriel came to him in a vision and told him to take his African American people back home to the Holy Land of Israel. In fact, a few thousand African Hebrew Israelites do live in their own community of Dimona, Israel.

The African Hebrew Israelites are part of a longer tradition that marries African-centered thought to religion. "Some of the most forceful twentieth-century theologies of black ethnicity appeared in the African American communities of Judaism and Islam" (Johnson 2010: 132). The Black Judaism of Wentworth Arthur Mathew and the Moorish Science Temple of America founded by Timothy Drew signaled a "new religious order that asserted blacks were people with peoplehood, with history and heritage that transcended the space and time of the American experience of slavery and racism" (Johnson 2010: 127). As do the Shrine of the Black Madonna and the Hebrew Israelites, these religious movements of the early 1900s asserted a black ethnic identity and posited that black Africans were the key figures in biblical history. Black Judaism and Black Islam, such as the Nation of Islam, have been derided as invented quasi religions and efforts that "usurped a false claim to the heritage of real Jews [or Muslims] as a means of political expediency and social protest" (Johnson 2010: 136). Others have pointed out that "all religions are invented" and that "all derive from intersubjective responses to and participation in political, economic, social and ideological realms" (Johnson 2010: 139).

I visited the African Hebrew Israelite congregation in Atlanta on several occasions and even attended a service led by Ben Ammi. In fact, I considered making this group the focus of my study, as I was intrigued by their principles promoting spirituality, healthy eating, and family integrity based on their understanding of African cultural ways. I was also fascinated by the willingness of so many to immigrate to Israel as well as troubled by their unapologetically patriarchal dynamics. However, while definitely incorporating much of the rhetoric and ideology of both Afrocentrism and black nationalism, the group did not discuss blackness in the same overt ways as did First Afrikan. This group was more concerned, in my opinion, with its "African-Jewish" cultural identity than its black identity.

Outside of Atlanta, one of the better-known Afrocentric congregations is Trinity United Church of Christ in Chicago, whose credo is "Unashamedly Black and Unapologetically Christian." Just as First Afrikan is part of the predominantly white Presbyterian Church, Trinity, with more than eight thousand members, is the largest congregation affiliated with the predominantly white United Church of Christ denomination. Also similar to First Afrikan, it serves a largely black middle class constituency and is staunchly Black Nationalist.

Trinity may be familiar because it was the church of Barack Obama and his former pastor, Jeremiah Wright. Reverend Wright is also connected to Reverend Lomax in that both received their doctorates from United Theological Seminary. United Theological is a United Methodist seminary in Ohio with coursework in African and African American studies as well as Womanist theology. Other notable alumni include Vashti Murphy McKenzie, the first female bishop in the African Methodist Episcopal Church; and Suzan Johnson Cook, an ambassador appointed by Barack Obama and the first female senior pastor in the American Baptist Church USA. Among the faculty have been Gayraud Wilmore, a noted black theologian, and Prathia Hall, a prominent womanist theologian. Perhaps because of this shared experience at United Theological, Wright and Lomax also share a theology that privileges Afrocentric thought, black liberation theology and Black Nationalist ideology.

Reverend Wright's Afrocentric and black liberation theology are evident in this excerpt:

> Come back with me in time, way back to a faraway place, and stand for a moment shoulder to shoulder with another people in another place, another time, and another predicament. . . . These are profound people, a proud people, and a praying people. . . . It was these people

who created the first cultures and developed the first civilizations on earth. It was these people, black of skin and wooly of hair, who gave the world Pythagorean mathematics and the cosmology of Thales of Miletus. . . . But something happened to these proud people. Stand here and listen . . . it sounds like they're in exile—snatched away from the homes they built, the places they lived and the sites they loved. . . . And in some places, no longer are they even considered human beings. . . . The song they sing sounds like a song sung from the bowels of exile. Listen to it: Sometimes I feel like a motherless child, a long way from home. (Wright 2007: 237–238)

In this passage, Wright draws connections between ancient and great African civilizations and enslaved African Americans. Later in the passage, he describes the biblical characters of Daniel, Shadrach, Meshach, and Abednego as African. These same biblical actors are pivotal in the Afrocentric theology of Reverends Lomax and Coleman. Reverend Wright writes that these were not the original names of the biblical actors but ones given to them during their time of exile. In another excerpt, he writes of exiled Africans and the names given to them while enslaved in the United States:

Negro, Negrito, Moreno, Negress, Nigra, Nigger, Colored, Black, Coons, Sambo, Jungle Bunny, Boy, Girl, Uncle, and Mammy. The empire stripped the exiles of their names and imposed its own names upon them so that five or six generations later the original names were lost to memory. . . . When you take away a person's name, you take away his or her history. (Wright 2007: 240)

Here, we see Reverend Wright's Black Nationalist leanings. His bombastic Black Nationalist critique is what focused such controversy upon him during the 2008 election. It was reported in the media that he had repeated Malcolm X's words that "America's chickens are coming home to roost" in response to the September 11 attacks. Theologian Dr. Jamie Phelps contends that "what Wright was saying was as long as we continue to be blind to the social injustice that is part of the US, then we are putting ourselves over and against the Gospel" (Markey 2008). However, others did not give his words such a generous interpretation.

Prior to this controversy, Reverend Wright was widely celebrated for Trinity United Church of Christ's social programs on behalf of the poor and disadvantaged. During his thirty-six-year tenure as the pastor, Reverend Wright advocated not only for ministry to the poor but their inclusion in the middle class congregation. He wrote, "Having a witness *among* the poor and having a ministry *to* the poor is one thing, but making the poor folks members of your congregation is something else altogether" (Wright 2007: 15).

As part of this perspective and in keeping with their Afrocentric ethos, Trinity makes economic contributions and visits to the community of Saltpond, Ghana. The church seeks to "help the town maintain and preserve local traditional values and systems" and to "provide opportunities for dialogue with African Christians as well as collaboration that supports empowered institutions in Africa" (Speller 2005: 96).

First Afrikan Presbyterian shares with the Shrine of the Black Madonna a reading of the Bible as a black text with Jesus as a black man, shares with the African Hebrew Israelites a promotion of African values and principles to enhance spirituality and family integrity, and shares with Trinity United Church of Christ a sensibility of itself as a middle class congregation with particular responsibilities to less-affluent African Americans.

And Presbyterian

First Afrikan is a member of the Greater Atlanta Presbytery, part of the western synod of the Presbyterian Church, USA. Presbyterians consider themselves unique in two ways: "They adhere to a pattern of religious thought known as Reformed theology and a form of government that stresses the active, representational leadership of both ministers and church members." According to its website (www.pcusa.org), the Presbyterian Church, USA, is the largest, most visible, and most influential Presbyterian denomination in North America and is 92 percent European American and 3 percent African American. Approximately two million people are members of the denomination, with Peachtree Presbyterian Church in Atlanta having the largest membership at nearly nine thousand. First Afrikan Presbyterian is a bit more modest in size, with a membership that fluctuates near seven hundred.

Reverend Lomax explained that the Presbyterian Church has placed considerable effort into nurturing racial and ethnic diversity among its congregants and therefore was open to this Afrocentric-themed church. Within the literature of First Afrikan, the clergy explain that the church is as Presbyterian as it is Afrocentric. For instance, any person considering joining the congregation is given the new members' class study book (Lomax 2002). Within it, the pastor defines what a Presbyterian is, provides early Presbyterian Church history, and explains the belief system and the organization of the Presbyterian Church. Worship service at First Afrikan adheres to the structure established by the denomination that generally includes prayer, music, Bible reading, and a sermon based upon scripture.

During my time at the church, some members discussed separating from the Presbyterian Church and establishing an independent Afrocentric denomination. If that were to happen, the church building and land would be relinquished to the Presbyterian Church. While there were conversations about separation during the time of my study, First Afrikan functioned as a Presbyterian congregation with Reverend Lomax appointed by the Presbyterian Church. Members of the church with whom I spoke understood themselves as belonging to a Presbyterian congregation and accepted Presbyterian rules of worship and governing. However, as mentioned earlier, this did not necessarily mean that they personally identified as Presbyterian.

Although First Afrikan was a Presbyterian Church, the Afrocentric bias was the more compelling reason for attending the church for most of the members with whom I interacted. In addition, most of the literature, including the new members' class study book, programs distributed during service, and the leadership transformation curriculum and education handbook privileged a discussion of Afrocentrism over Presbyterianism. For example, after the discussion of Presbyterianism, in the new members' class study book is the following excerpt:

As Africentric Christians, we see no conflict between our culture(s) and the Christ. We, like Jesus, are both African and believers in God. Further, we claim the Bible as an authentic African document. In it, we find the story of how a liberating God set an ethnically diverse African people free from the bondage of slavery. We also have the story of an African messiah called of God to return to Egypt, Africa before beginning his public ministry in Judea and the Galilee. We have been intentional about using expressions and stories that reflect and authenticate our histories and cultures as Africans and as Christians. (Lomax 2002: 24)

Thus, while operationally a Presbyterian church, in spirit First Afrikan is Afrocentric. The next chapter focuses on how Afrocentrism is defined and integrated into understandings of self and enacted through bodily and linguistic behaviors by the members of First Afrikan. Church members explain what it means to them to have an Afrocentric consciousness, how they understand their relationship to the continent of Africa, and the meaning for them of adopting African hairstyles, dress and names—as well as why some have chosen not to do so.

2

Situating the Self

Becoming Afrikan in America

Afrocentric Consciousness

I met with Carmen at one of the grocery stores in Lithonia. In her thirties, with creamy deep brown skin and short cropped reddish brown hair, Carmen worked as a quality-control manager for a chain of markets. Amid the din of clanging shopping carts, chattering children, and announcements concerning frozen peas, we talked about what Afrocentrism meant to her.

"All right," I asked, "do you consider yourself to be Afrocentric?"

"Well, up until about four weeks ago, no," responded Carmen.

"Why is that?" I inquired.

"Because I really didn't identify with anything, to be honest with you. I mean, I was black and I knew that I couldn't get away from it. I didn't like being black sometimes, I will be honest about that. And I didn't really have a consciousness, which I still don't have a full consciousness of."

"What do you mean—a full consciousness of it?"

"I didn't know what it really meant to be black outside of what I've been doing for thirty-one years. I remember saying all the time that I envied people who were of the Jewish faith. I envied people who were of the Islamic faith only because they were living their way of life, and it seemed so often that, you know, us, black people, we just really just kind of did whatever. We never really had a way of life and that kind of didn't make a difference to me at first. It really didn't because I didn't think it mattered. But the more I got into going to the church, the more I realized I really didn't know who I was, and I was being in denial about how much it really meant to be an African."

Until Bible study classes at First Afrikan, blackness was problematic for Carmen because there did not seem to be a coherent sense of culture except for that associated with negative images. Furthermore, the African part of African American had not meant much to her as she did not feel a real connection to the continent or culture in the same way that she imagined Jewish and Islamic peoples did to their homelands and cultures. However, for Carmen, the Afrocentric community provided the longed for sense of belonging to a group with a long and proud history as well as a rich contemporary culture.

In contrast, Felicia Prince connected with Africa as a teenager when her family hosted an exchange student from the Ivory Coast. He spoke to Felicia of his village and taught her some of his native language. She recalled most clearly how he cooked for the family, serving the main dish in a large bowl in the middle of the table from which they all ate. "We would do everything the way they would do it over there." Felicia explained that this experience of cultural exchange was pivotal in cementing her interest in African culture and was not incidental to her choice to marry a man with a strong Afrocentric consciousness.

People in my study tended to follow one of four paths to an Afrocentric identity. Carmen did not have much awareness of Afrocentrism until encountering First Afrikan, where she was awakened to a feeling of connection with African culture. Interestingly, two people insisted that they had been African-centered since childhood and that, in fact, this awareness set them apart in their families and communities. For these two, it was not that anyone taught or influenced them but, rather, that their Africanness was innate and had naturally made itself apparent in their consciousness. More often, however, members' experiences were like Felicia's, and people were introduced to African culture during childhood by a parent or another person. For the fourth group, it was participation in the Civil Rights movement and the Black Is Beautiful era as a teenager or young adult that fomented an individual's interest in an African-centered identity. Those who were inculcated with an African sensibility either by a significant person in their lives or through participation in the black empowerment movement constituted most of my study population.

No matter the path to Afrocentrism, most people emphasized that an African-centered consciousness was intrinsic to an Afrocentric identity. It was repeatedly explained to me that Afrocentrism was first, and foremost, a state of mind, a particular type of awareness. For example, one person defined Afrocentrism in the following way: "So for me Afrocentric or Afrocentrism is once you've understood who you are and can accept that, you start seeing the world through that realm, through that lens. So it's how you see the world and how you expect the world to some extent to treat you." In this definition, as in the next, there is the contention that an Afrocentric consciousness is an awareness of an authentic and true identity that was present all along even if unrecognized. As David explained, "How would I define it? Let's see. I would define it as a true sense of knowing who you are, knowing where you come from, and being proud of it."

Another member explained that, once an individual better understood herself, it was incumbent upon her to behave differently. Catherine defined Afrocentrism as "a deep level of understanding of yourself and accepting your culture and embracing it and letting the world know that this is me, this is who I am, and infusing it into every part of your life and just everything. It is, I know, it's real deep."

This sentiment was echoed by Jerome Kent. Jerome was raised by a mother that he described without hesitation as Afrocentric but who did not apply the term to herself. His wife Nina explained that her Afrocentric consciousness was nurtured by both Jerome and his mother. It is this shared consciousness that Jerome feels holds them together as a couple:

> I think one of the biggest bonds we have as a couple is the fact that we're very open and giving. And you know, I think that that has a lot to do with Afrocentrism as far as, how do I put it? Let's just say that, I believe that since everything comes from Africa, that we all do have some kind

of connection, and so I feed on that connection, and I give that connection to everybody. We both just really, like our jobs, you know. And on the side, she mentors young black women, basically in high school, and I have my own tutoring service and mentoring service on the side, as well. Our lives have to do with community and it's an I/we philosophy—you know that we're all in this together.

For Jerome and Nina being Afrocentric is not just identifying with African cultural practices but enacting certain principles in their everyday lives such as engaging conscientiously with the community. It was intrinsic to their understanding of themselves as Afrocentric that they mentored other young African Americans by not only helping them to do better in school but by instilling, at a young age, a pride in being black and an awareness of a connection to Africa.

Valerie Owens also emphasized mentoring and community. She described an incident at the hospital where she works where one day younger, male coworkers were overheard referring to a woman as a "chick." Valerie felt it her duty to educate them as to why it was inappropriate to refer to a woman in that manner and more appropriate to use the woman's given name. "We can't call each other chick and stuff like that. We have to be respectful of each other and call each other by our names." One of the young men, who she refers to as her little brother, respectfully listened and promised to change his ways. When he thanked her for the insight, she replied, "I am always looking out for you. I have to help us teach, learn about each other, and how we're supposed to treat each other." Valerie explained to me, "That is what Afrocentricity is. It's not how you dress or anything like that. Just being respectful of each other, and don't let anyone else disrespect someone who looks like you. And if you see an injustice, if you can, try to fix it."

Of note, only five of the thirty people with whom I spoke used the term "Afrocentric" before coming to the church. Everyone but Carmen understood themselves to have had an Afrocentric consciousness long before joining the congregation in that they took pride in their African-ness, sought to learn more about Africa, and engaged in practices that they considered culturally African, but significantly they did not use the term in reference to themselves. For some, it was because they were unaware of the term, and, for others, they had not realized how relevant it was to their understanding of self until it was explained by Reverend Lomax.

This chapter describes how an Afrocentric consciousness manifests in behavior as exemplified through dress codes and hair styling as well as naming and racial/ethnic labeling practices. In addition, the relationship that people have with the African continent is examined. Of interest are the varied ways through which individuals make meaning in their lives through their performance of Afrocentrism.

Sartorial, Coiffured, and Linguistic Acts

Evelyn is forty-nine years old, slender with warm brown skin and hip-length locks. I met with her on a Friday afternoon at her house in Stone Mountain to discuss how she felt about being black:

> It took a long road for me. Because growing up, being black was not a good thing—even in my household. And it was always a negative connotation to being black. My grandmother raised me where if you are black you will never amount to anything. She believed there is a only a certain level that you can reach and it's really not that high. But I always rebelled against that. And I just wanted something. I knew there was something better but I didn't know quite what it was.

She leaned back and crossed her legs as she recalled a transformational experience in high school. At sixteen, Evelyn became part of a program that helped orient students as they prepared to go to predominantly white schools. "And it was there that I learned that there was a positiveness about being black. And that I learned that you didn't have to conform to the European. You could be yourself. You could be with them but don't take on what they do."

Because of this experience in high school, Evelyn was particularly excited about her move to Atlanta in her thirties. "I heard about all the blacks in high positions in politics and who owned things and were doing things for the community. I felt this would be the place for me. But I was disappointed by the disconnectedness among black people."

The expression upon her face was a mixture of sadness and frustration as she explained her belief that people prized power, money, and individual needs above the community. Although African Americans had a measure of political and economic power in Atlanta, to Evelyn, they did not have sufficient pride in their heritage.

"How would you describe your heritage?" I asked. "How do you define your racial and ethnic identity?"

"I say African American. But I want to change that on those little forms. They give you the choice—African American and whatever and whatever. From now on, I'm going to go to put African."

I was taken aback by this response. While I expected an answer that privileged her African heritage, I did not expect her to identify only that aspect of her genetic and cultural background.

"Why?" I asked.

"I feel I'm an African. I'm of African descent living here in America."

"Do you think that your Africanness is the same as someone who actually lives in Africa?" I pushed.

"No, it isn't because, just in being in Senegal and Mali, they are so very different. Their being different is that they have, in essence, materially nothing, but they appear to be the happiest people, and they have what they need. And I look at us here in America, and we have everything at our fingertips, and we're not happy, and we always want more. I could easily give this up and live in Africa. And learn how to live the way they live."

Evelyn's argument was that cultural behaviors were different between persons of African descent in the United States and persons of African descent in Africa. However, importantly to her, despite the cultural differences, there was a shared African essence that justified her identifying as African. Nonetheless, she believed that the cultural behaviors and practices of those living in Africa were more authentic, and she sought to incorporate them into her life.

In her quest to become more authentically African, Evelyn explained that she had two types of clothing—her work uniform and her African clothing, both of which she wore to work.

"How is wearing the Afrocentric clothing received at the hospital?" I asked.

"They are used to me now. Before they thought I was going somewhere, and I said no, this is what I wear. I tell them, I don't buy European clothes. I used to wear European clothes but I wanted to get up to where everything in my wardrobe is Afrocentric."

In addition to her changed wardrobe, Evelyn changed her hairstyle. She began wearing locks in 2000. In response to my question of why she chose locks, Evelyn explained, "Because I wanted to do something different. It was the new millennium. And I said that I wanted to do something different to be unique to me. At that time in 2000 at First Afrikan quite a few people had locks."

"How important do you think the clothing and the hairstyles are to a sense of African identity?" I asked.

"I think it has quite a lot to do with it because once you put that combination together, you're making a statement. And I think it kinda ironic, nothing bad about it, just ironic, that you would have locks and you're in a three-piece suit. There's just something that's not right with that picture. It's like you want to be yourself but you can't get there yet. Like you still have to play a part. Like you're still living a dichotomy."

"What other things do you think are important to living in an Afrocentric way?"

"Reading and learning more about the African culture. And incorporating those things into your life. "

"Does it affect your diet?" I asked.

"It should, but it doesn't," she responded with a sheepish laugh.

Like Evelyn, many First Afrikan church members adopt African dress, natural hairstyles, and change the labels they use to identify themselves ethnically. For them, to do so is to reject European ways of being that are considered imposed as well as alienating and to reconnect with African ways of being that are considered right and natural for a person of African descent. However, not all of the members found the need to wear boubous, grow locks, or change their ethnic labels. Three of the women that I interviewed had permed hair and said that they did not feel it in anyway took from their Africanness as it was just a way of wearing their hair. While everyone with whom I spoke had at least one Afrocentric piece of clothing, many did not feel it necessary to wear those pieces regularly as they defined true Afrocentric consciousness as being manifest in behavior toward others rather than in clothing. More than half of the people had shifted from calling themselves "African Americans" to referring to themselves as "Afrikans in

America" or "Afrikan." These were ways through which they hoped to reinforce within their consciousnesses, and the consciousnesses of others, the primacy of Africanness in their identities.

Dress, hair, and language are important aspects of an evolving Afrocentric identity. A consideration of the ways these practices act as important markers of identity should provide insight into the varied ways that individuals negotiate Afrocentrism.

African Dress

The donning of kente cloth is the sartorial act most identified with Afrocentrism. A royal cloth in Ghana, it entered the consciousness of African Americans in the 1964 when Muhammad Ali was shown wearing it in an *Ebony* magazine pictorial during his trip to Africa. In the 1990s, it became especially popular as a marker of Africanness, as evidenced by Bill and Hillary Clinton, who wore it during their 1998 trip to various African countries (Ross 1998). One can see kente prints throughout First Afrikan Church, both as pieces of art and on members' clothing. At the church, what struck me most was not that many people wore mainstream clothing with Afrocentric accents, such as kente designs, on the pockets or stoles across the shoulders. Rather, what struck me was that, if people were not dressed in conventional dress with perhaps some African jewelry, they were most likely to have on full African dress. Furthermore, when I asked people about their Afrocentric clothing, they responded by talking about their *African* clothing. Therefore it is important to note the congregation's distinction between *Afrocentric* clothing as being American-style clothing with accents such as kente print and *African* clothing as that which is actually made in Africa or in the United States by an African seamstress.

Dress is significant because "it both touches the body and faces outward toward others," and it "becomes a flash point of conflicting values, fueling contests in historical encounters, in interactions across class, between genders and generations, and in recent global cultural and economic exchanges" (Hansen 2004: 372). Clothing in African America, as in other marginalized communities, "lends an alternative route to status attainment by controlling how others gaze, by resisting mainstream notions of appearance, by providing a place where one can exert the power of expression resulting in creative, unique and novel appearance and by gaining power by visibly and politically resisting mainstream society" (Hansen 2004: 31). In her dissertation on middle class black aesthetics, Carol Lynette Hall (1994: 58) contends that African Americans "have retained a flair from African culture for aesthetics, style and self-expression displayed via clothing and personal adornment. The affinity for high affect colors, style or individual expression, improvisation and exotic features and the tendency to dress up combine with metaphysical beliefs and a unified spirit." In other words, dress is significant because it is a medium through which the oppressed can subvert the dominant ideology by invoking different standards of taste, and it is a means through which ethnic identity is preserved and creatively expressed. For many members of the church, African clothing is salient as an overt expression of their rejection of Eurocentric culture and as an outward display of their internal Africanness.

African clothing is a significant part of Frances Wilcox's identity. "I dress mostly in African clothes. I do wear Western-style clothes if they're very colorful. I'm an African diva even though you can't tell that today. I love to be beautiful, and I love to dress very nice." In contrast, Carter Langford has not worn African clothing often but is now purchasing more pieces:

I'm getting into it. To me, it's a message. I work around a lot of white people. I like psychologically messing with people and I think when you walk in with African clothing, to some black people it makes them uncomfortable because they're saying, "Uh-oh, here he comes, he's a rebel." To white people it's like, "Oh." For a lot of white people, it's almost like you're challenging their authority. When you walk in wearing African clothing in a formal or informal setting, I think a lot of white people just get intimidated by that, or it makes them uncomfortable because you're acknowledging your Africanness, and a lot of them feel guilty still, especially your liberal whites, when they see that, and I think that's good. I like that.

Carter's glee at raising the ire of his coworkers can certainly be viewed as an act of subversion and resistance. That white supervisors and coworkers were not always comfortable with or sure of how to respond to African dress was substantiated in the experience of Nina Kent when she wore her hair covered in a traditional African headwrap:

> We had a new CFO come to the company, and I wore my headdress one day. And I walk in and sit down at my desk. He comes in, he says, "You look very historical." So I already knew where he was going with that. So I'm like, "Well what do you mean?" because I want to have him say it. He was like, "You look . . . I don't want to say it." I said, "No. Say it, just go." He said, "Well, like you look like Mammy." I was like, "Really." So, my day goes on and he—I just take it all in because I'm like shocked. I didn't expect to hear it, but then again, maybe I should have. But I'm walking down the hall and he casually said, "Hey Mammy," and someone else hears it and takes it to HR. And he, like, apologized to me, but at the same time, he didn't really mean it because he felt that since it was in a joking manner I shouldn't have taken it to heart like that, like it wasn't a racial thing.

Nina explains that the event made her even more dedicated to wearing African clothing to work. For Catherine McBride, African clothes are not just about interracial dynamics but speak to something more personal and spiritual:

> When there are times I know are going to be uphill battles, I mentally prepare. There is something about just getting dressed and looking in the mirror and looking at myself and being dressed in Afrocentric clothing or something that I actually bought when I was in Africa and putting that on and coming to deal with situations. It's almost— it's like calming myself. It's like a piece of my ancestors are with me all the time. It's like putting on their clothes. And it's really empowering and calming all at the same time. It's like being at peace.

However, some did not wear any African clothing at all, to work or otherwise. While they might have some African jewelry or mainstream clothing with some Afrocentric accent, African clothing was more elusive. Denise Payne explains, "I can't afford it. I just truly can't afford it. I refuse to wear African clothes made in China. So if I could afford it, I would wear it." It was explained to me by another woman that African dresses can cost from $300 to $500 or more, although pieces could be purchased for less than $100, "but that would be like shopping at Target as opposed to Parisian." Many of the women bought clothing at the different shops in the West End of Atlanta that specialize in them, or from the trunks of cars of African designers now living in the United States, or during their trips to an African country. Some of the women of First Afrikan participate in networks where they are able to learn about good deals or to exchange outfits between them.

Pressed and Locked

African American hair textures and styles "index broader, racialized epistemological and ontological structures that frame the construction and maintenance of racial categories. Hair texture and the ways it is imagined, discussed and manipulated, in historical and contemporary contexts, speaks to the very phenomenology of race itself" (Russell 2002: 22). In addition, hair is read in particular ways in terms of gender in that "uncontrolled hair, indexing unbridled nature, functioned metonymically to symbolize women themselves as organic, expressing emotionality and sensuality" (Russell 2002: 75). Consequently, when African American women talk about the natural state of their hair, it is often in terms of controlling it and reigning it in, with an end effect often approximating that of European American women's hair: smooth and straight.

Hadiya Hunter, an attractive woman completing her doctorate in education, has long hair that she wears pressed. Pressing hair is a way of straightening the hair with heat but is neither permanent nor as damaging as chemical straightening. Hadiya explained that her hair was permed or straightened with chemicals when she was nine because it was so thick and difficult to control. In her twenties, as her Afrocentric consciousness developed, she decided to go natural with her hair and so cut it and wore it short. As it grew, she experimented with different natural styles, such as braids, twists, and afro puffs, until last year when she decided to press it and dye it a reddish brown. Part of her reason for pressing her hair was that she just wanted a change from the other styles, and part of her reason was that it was easier to manage the length and thickness of her hair. That Hadiya refers to both the pressing and perming of her hair as an easier way to *manage* its thickness speaks to Russell's argument that women are socialized to feel that they must tame the natural state of their hair.

While both white and black women are bombarded by advertising for products to help them control their hair, there is an additional component with regard to African-descended women's naturally coily or nappy hair: "Scholars have clearly established that nappy hair texture is the most potent indicator of an improperly socialized and physically unappealing body in American society. Though nappy refers specifically to hair, it is a metaphor for the idea that blackness in general is essentially dirty, disorderly, unrefined and in need of cultivation" (Russell 2002: 38). It was understood by the congregants that part of an Afrocentric consciousness is to refute these ideas by celebrating the natural textures of one's hair. Rather than being seen as problematic, the coily nature of black hair is seen as powerful and as an organic refutation of European dominance. Nearly half of the women at First Afrikan wear twists, locks, and other decidedly unstraight styles. These women celebrated their coily hair as being one of the most African aspects of themselves. According to Russell, for many African Americans women,

> Like the spirits of Africans and African Americans themselves, the nap is imbued with the power to stomp, kick and sneak around all historical attempts to mess with it, to break down its natural essence and succumb to alteration. Sent by divine force, the nap is in effect, the very essence of God, sent by God to defy attempts, even those self imposed, to control the Black body. (2002: 40)

When Hadiya pressed her hair, some members of the congregation were taken aback by this choice because, although pressing hair is technically considered natural as there are no chemicals applied, it is also considered problematic as there is no way to distinguish it from permed hair just by looking and because it conforms to European standards of beauty. Hadiya confided that she felt as if she were cheating a little in terms of her Afrocentrism by choosing to press her hair. But, she pointed out, she did not only wear her pressed hair in standard curled styles but also arranged it in more African configurations.

The connection between coily hair and Africanness was made most clear when I spoke with Amelia Douglas. Fifty-six years of age, Mrs. Douglas is a light-skinned woman with light brown eyes, and her hair is naturally straight, which she wears in a short cap about her face. During my conversation with her over an evening meal of pancakes at the local pancake house, she lamented how she had been unsuccessful in her several attempts to lock her hair. She was frustrated by the refusal of her silken curls to conform to the locking process as did more coily hair, and she asserted that she had not yet given up.

However, not only African American women attempt to control or celebrate the texture of their hair. A professional look for black men is a short, low-cut style that happens to deemphasize the curl of their hair. In addition, there are several products on the market to help men relax the coil of their hair so that it appears wavy or straight. Unfortunately, there is much less research concerning black men as their "stylistic practices are rarely subjected to the kind of critical scrutiny that women's practices are simply because within patriarchal contexts, open concern with hair and style are thought not to be the province of heterosexual men" (Russell 2002: 230). However, men did speak with me about their choice to buck Eurocentric standards and to grow locks or big afros.

David Parsons is forty-five years old and has shoulder-length locks that are made ever more elegant by the gentle silvering of his hair. Once he decided to adopt an Afrocentric lifestyle, locks were an aspect of that, but he was not quite prepared for the negative reactions from both black and white peers. Significantly, that reaction reinforced for him that locks were a potent way to resist the influence of Eurocentrism and to demonstrate his changed consciousness:

> A lot of people could not understand why I began to wear locks. And one of my things, I said that it was an outward manifestation of what was happening on the inside. I wore my hair short because I thought it was the acceptable way of being in this world. And when I began to wear my locks, I saw how people treated me differently. And I said, "You mean to tell me just because I'm wearing my hair differently, people began to look at me and treat me differently?" So I began to see how people really thought about me. As long as I looked like everyone else and acted like

everyone else, I was fine. But when I began to try to display who I am through my dress and through my hair, then there was an issue. "Why you got to do all that. It don't take all that to be black, to be African." But it's okay when I wore my shirt and tie to work because I am with the status quo, but when I wore this garb to work, then there would be questions.

I Call Myself

While choices concerning dress and hair styling are integral to how many church members navigate a sense of Afrocentric identity, there is yet an even more personal question that must be negotiated: What do I call myself?

For many, changing one's name to one of African origin is considered a vital step toward a more African-centered consciousness. Within the many discourses concerning identity at First Afrikan, one of the most prominent is the emphasis on language and the ways through which it shapes consciousness. As Reverend Coleman explained:

> It's an important part of any identity because to me language shapes reality. It's through language we get the primary codes, symbols that inform our consciousness and form what we think, how we think and forms how we behave. Because I know that many of us are not speaking our indigenous languages. We are speaking languages that have been imposed upon us through the enslavement of our ancestors. So, the original languages that we might have spoken are lost. So with respect to African American identity, I try in my own training and present avocation to help us reshape our identity as African Americans and as African American Christians through coming to terms with a closer understanding of the original languages.

Therefore, having an African name is one of the most powerful and intimate symbols of a an Afrocentric consciousness.

The means through which individuals acquired an African name varied. Hadiya Hunter's name was given to her at birth by her parents. Anaya Duvant changed her first name based on a character in a movie that celebrated Africanness, and Ebele Kuumba was given her name by her husband. One of the most interesting name change processes was that of Onaedo Odun, who visited an African village that had been recreated in North Georgia. The chief performed a reading using cowrie shells and divined not only that her family was from Ghana but also that, had she been born in Africa, her name would have been Onaedo.

Catherine McBride used to have an African name but learned at First Afrikan that she had not followed the proper path toward choosing it. Consequently, she returned to her birth name:

> Well, you know, I went about choosing one, but it wasn't done properly, so I don't consider that. I will have one, but I want to do it the proper way. It's almost like someone does a reading, a reading can be done on you, and through that reading certain attributes are associated. And then someone can look within and look at what best suits you for who you are. And when I did it before it was like in a workshop and looking at books, and you look up the names and look up the meaning, whatever, whatever. But I want it to be more of a spiritual exercise. More than me just looking at a book because I'm in the middle of a workshop.

It was explained to me that a name should reflect a person's nature and that renaming the self is a spiritual process, therefore once a person has reached a certain level of consciousness, an elder who knows her well will choose a name that appropriately reflects the person's spirit.

Frances Wilcox plans to change her name, too, although she has mixed feelings about doing so:

> Yeah, I've thought about it, but, there's a little catch. I also really love my name. It was also was my father's name, and I loved him so much. It would feel as if I were losing something, even though I know intellectually that I do need an African name—because I need to rename myself from the source. Because we are without that connection by not using our own language. I feel I'd be closing the gap when I would correct some of that kind of thing.

Carter Langford has decided not to change his name. "Everyone knows me as Carter. I'm very comfortable with Carter. So for that reason, I don't think I would adopt one." However, most of those with whom I spoke wanted an African name and were waiting for an elder to give one to them.

Deciding whether or not to change his first and last names was only one of the choices that awaited a person when creating an Afrocentric identity. Church members were also quite self-conscious of how to identify their ethnic identity and, consequently, the term "African American" was a complicated one.

By Any Other Name

According to Tom W. Smith, "racial labels have been of special importance to Black Americans. Wrenched from their native lands, Blacks lost their core personal identities" (1992: 496). However, they soon engaged in efforts to forge a new culture in a new land, as well as to build social institutions that served their needs and promoted their interests. Unfortunately, the autonomy of these efforts was continually thwarted by "White society, which strictly controlled Blacks and sought to shape and to regulate Black status and consciousness" (Smith 1992: 496). A particular site of contestation between blacks and whites has been that of racial labeling, as whites have tended to impose pejorative terms. In response, blacks have adopted various racial labels to define themselves as a people with "the common goal to find a group label that instilled group pride and consciousness" (Smith 1992: 497).

In his research on racial labels, Smith found that "Colored" was the dominant term adopted by black people in the mid- to late nineteenth century. Used by both blacks and others, it was considered an inclusive term covering mulattos and others of mixed ancestry, as well as those with complete black ancestry. While "Colored" tended to be more popular among the more established communities of black people, "Negro" was preferred by Civil War freedmen. In addition, "Negro" was considered more grammatically versatile, usable as both adjective and noun and in the singular and plural; however, it was often used as a term of reproach by whites and further suffered from its association to racial epithets. Even so, for a period, "Negro" was considered an empowering label. "Racial progress and the hopes and aspirations of Blacks were to be captured by the term Negro. For a short spell, the term Negro occupied roughly the same place as the words Black and African American occupy today" (Smith 1992: 497).

Then in the late 1950s and early 1960s, in order to break from the past and to shed remnants of slavery and racial serfdom, a new name was chosen. "Black" was promoted as standing for racial pride, militancy, power, and rejection of the status quo. Initially favored by radicals and militants, "black" was used to describe those who were progressive, while "Negro" was for those more established and identified with the status quo. "Black" was also chosen as a deliberate antithesis to white, but it also had negative connotations of evil (Smith 1992: 501).

In 1988, the emphasis was to shift from choosing the appropriate racial label to naming a burgeoning ethnic identity. Jesse Jackson championed "African American" as a replacement for "black" as the term was argued to have cultural integrity and to be an avenue to put the group on a parallel level with white ethnic groups. As Jackson explained, "To be called African American has cultural integrity. It puts us in our proper historical context. Every ethnic group in this country has a reference to some land base, some historical cultural base. African Americans have hit that level of cultural maturity. There are Armenian-Americans and Jewish-Americans and Arab-Americans and Italian-American; and with a degree of accepted and reasonable pride, they connect their heritage to their mother country and where they are now" (Martin 1991: 83).

Jackson's campaign for an ethnic label emerged during a period when Native Americans were winning significant legal battles concerning tribal lands and when Japanese Americans had received reparations for World War II internments. Martin contends that, in part, "the announcement of African American ethnicity was a reassertion of the primacy of Black moral claims" and that the "cultural offensive to build an African American identity renewed the attack on that lingering false consciousness embedded in a social structure of racial oppression" (1991: 88). By crafting a more self-conscious ethnic identity, as opposed to the battle-weary racial identity, African Americans hoped to compete on more even footing with other groups. "In a multi-cultural America, where inequalities based on race and class are obscured under the neutral term of ethnicity, and where struggles for representation and access to resources are increasingly fought on the basis of ethnic allegiance, it is through the display of an ethnic identity that African Americans as a cultural group seemingly acquire access to citizenship" (Hernandez-Reguant 1999: 101).

During my participant observation at First Afrikan, I heard people refer to themselves as "African American." But, several individuals also called themselves an "Afrikan in America" or an "Afrikan." Hoping to understand what the distinction was between these labels and on what basis a person chose between them, I chose this as one of the first questions I asked participants during an interview.

The procedure for asking participants to identify themselves racially or ethnically was to pose the question, and if there was hesitation or confusion, I would offer examples. "Do you call yourself Black, Black American, African American, Afrikan in America or Afrikan?" I asked. No one ever answered "Black" or "Black American," although each person used blackness in reference to themselves numerous times during our conversations. People either answered "Afrikan," "Afrikan in America," or "African American." The first response, "Afrikan," privileges Africanness and demonstrates an ambivalence toward, if not an outright rejection of, Americanness.

The second response, "Afrikan in America," distinguished between an African cultural identity and an African identity colored by American culture, those so labeled claiming the latter. It was also used to suggest a state of being displaced and a sense of alienation. Afrikans in America were not in the place they were supposed to be. Those calling themselves African Americans either took pride in their Americanness, not equating it with whiteness, or had resigned themselves to their Americanness.

When I asked Jerome Kent what terms he used to define his racial and or ethnic identity, he responded immediately, "I call myself African." Then, he paused, reflected for a moment, and then subtly squaring his shoulders, repeated, "I call myself African. I am here in America, but I relate more to the ancestral side of myself, and I'm still—I feel like I'm still speaking with—through African lips, so I call myself African."

"Okay, do you see a distinction between being African in *Africa* and African in *America*?"

"Oh, definitely, yeah. Yeah, I mean, in that respect, I would call myself African-American. You know, in my heart of heart, soul of souls, I call myself African, but for the most part, yeah, I mean, I was raised here in America and I have a lot of American thoughts and feelings inside, too. So, yeah, I mean, I guess that does—that is part of my makeup."

I posed the same question to Frances Wilcox, who joined the church within the past year.

"I recently classified myself as an Afrikan in America," she told me.

"Why Afrikan *in* America?" was my next question.

"Um, because first and foremost I feel African. America just seems like it's a place that I have been raised, and I've been, you know. That's where I live but, in my soul and my heart, I feel Afrikan."

"What did you call yourself before?"

"African American and before that Black. Never Negro. Never Colored."

"Alright. Is there a difference between African in Africa and being African in America?"

"Yes. Um, different because I live in America and I've been educated by the Western system so, of course, that is a product of my psyche you know, as opposed to having been born and raised in Africa with a real view of Africa. I'm learning the real view of Africa, but that's not my original mindset, so I think that is why it is different. And, well, the racism has a lot to do with it, too. Because as I said, when I was very young, I realized the difference because of my skin tone. And in Africa, I just have a sense that they've, even though I know that they have been colonized as well, but I think they have a more sense of who they are and where they come from."

Both Jerome and Frances had been members of First Afrikan for fewer than two years, and both had called themselves African American before joining the congregation. As a part of their evolving consciousness, it became imperative to each of them to emphasize their Africanness through the words that they used to identify themselves. However, this was an identity in some flux, as each wrestled with what their Africanness meant in the context of the United States as opposed to within the continent of Africa. For both, there was a sense that their Africanness was a given, an intrinsic aspect of their being, inherited along with the shade of their skin and the texture of their hair. Another congregant, Anaya Duvant, described Africanness as "a tie, a connection that you have that goes all the way back to the very beginning. To have a strong sense of pride and or your origins. Knowing your origins, or if you don't know it, try to learn it and—and just being what it is that is inherent to you."

And yet, there was the acknowledgment that Africanness has a learned aspect, as well, as their Africanness in the United States differed from the Africanness of peoples on the continent because their historical and contemporary experiences differed. I detected a quiet envy of the *African* Africanness, as it was perceived as being purer and less corrupted by European influence, although people acknowledged the effects of colonialism and postcolonialism in Africa. Attendant to this was a somber resignation toward having to be part American. In this context, the disdain was not so much a statement of their lack of patriotism or a critique of the political economic structure as much as it was a conflation of Americanness with whiteness and Europeanness.

For most congregants, while Africanness is important, they allowed that there were important cultural distinctions between Africanness and African Americanness. In addition, the actual phrasing changed depending upon the context. Catherine McBride provides an example of this:

> Depends on the situation. Here, on an application or whatever, I will put African American, but when I talk, I speak of myself as being of African descent. So it depends on what I'm actually doing and what's the purpose and what it is. But whatever it is, the fact that I'm African comes out someplace.

Home Is Where the Heart Is

As Africa is so central to these constructions of identity, I had the church members speak to me of their experience and conception of Africa. What I found was that about one third of the people with whom I spoke had traveled to at least one country, and the remaining wanted to visit in the near future. I would not describe any of them as being overly romantic, as many felt an ambivalence about living there on a permanent basis, and most were aware of the affect of colonialism upon the cultures.

For example, Valerie has been to Senegal and Mali and feels that she could live in either country. However, she would prefer to live in the place from which her ancestors originated and laments that she does not know where that is:

> That's what I'd really like to know—where, where did my ancestor come from in Africa. Well, I used to feel at a loss. Because other people, Europeans, they could always tell you where they came from. And they can tell you, "I was born here, and my parents came from here, and my great grandparents came from here, and we came to Ellis Island, and da da da, and da da da da." And that's like a loss because I don't know where we come from.

Frances Wilcox, a woman in her fifties with a mound of locks upon her head, has been to Gambia and Nigeria. Upon her first visit, she arrived with quite idealistic expectations:

> Basically, you know when I went to Africa, I had these preexisting notions of what would happen. I thought that when I got off the airplane that I was going to fall on the ground and start weeping and wailing and, just you know, just really being emotional. But that didn't happen. And at that time, when that didn't happen, I was kind of rethinking, you know, is this really what I thought it would be? Well you know Africa, it doesn't go by what you think.

But for Anaya Duvant, a Jamaican American woman, traveling to Ghana was life changing:

> It was like—it's like another extension, a transformation. For me, when I got there I felt I was home. Except the people spoke a different language. It was good for me to go to the capital of the Ashanti kingdom. And I had some spiritual experiences there. Overall, I would say that that deep yearning I had inside to make it to the Motherland, that going to Ghana satisfied that for me. In one respect it satisfied it. In another sense, it created a deeper yearning for me to go back because I connected so much, especially with the Ashanti. So it makes me wonder if somewhere deep down if that's not a part of my lineage, you know. So now I'm on that search.

For Valerie, Frances, and Anaya, going to Africa represented, in part, an opportunity to reconnect with the places where their ancestors were born and to return to where they believed they themselves were supposed to be. This is undoubtedly a romantic notion, but it was a romance sullied for Valerie by not knowing where home was and, for Frances, of not feeling at home once she got there. For Anaya, although she felt that she had made it to the right home, she was distressed by the state of the place:

> But I was very, very astounded by just how colonized Africans in Africa were. Sometimes we glorify Africa. And then like when I got there, I said, "My God, these people are—they're the same like us." Because when you see your sisters in Africa trying to bleach their skin, you know. I would see my sisters in the beautiful dresses, but they all had straight hair, you know. So a lot of the problems that we encounter here on this continent are being encountered there, too. So it's a huge problem in Africa, also. I remember driving around in the taxis, the back of it you see the picture of the white Jesus. And it really blew my mind. My God, am I in Africa or am I in America, you know?

While many who had been to Africa said that they would like to live there permanently, most voiced a similar dismay in how Eurocentric it seemed to be. The irony of returning home in order to rediscover their basic Africanness while those in Africa seemed to be moving toward ever-more European ways of being was profoundly disappointing for them. Nevertheless, Africa remained home in their hearts, and they had to at least visit once in their lifetimes.

Conclusion

For members of First Afrikan, Afrocentrism is understood as an avenue to remember and reconstruct a cultural identity that was undermined, although not completely lost, because of forced migration and slavery. This cultural identity privileges an awareness of the self as essentially African and, for many, requires the performance of certain behaviors, such as changes to appearance and naming practices. By wearing natural hairstyles such as braids and locks, donning African clothing, and travelling to Ghana or Senegal, members signal their conversion toward a more African-centered consciousness. The member is publicly declaring her sense of identity as well as solidarity with the larger group identity by adopting the group's code of how to properly live as an Afrocentric person. By calling himself something different, such as "Afrikan in America" rather than "African American," a church member announces seeing himself differently and asserts a desire to have this difference recognized by others. The practice of these rituals indicates that members have experienced a shift in identity.

Significantly, this shift in identity did not mean the person felt that the essence of his identity has been altered in any way. He was as he had always been—an African-descended individual who was meant to perceive the world and behave in the world in African ways. The difference was his new awareness of this destiny and his knowledge of how to act upon it. In other words, the change was a shift to an awareness of his authentic self.

Although the person did not consider the essence of his authentic identity to have changed, he nevertheless considered himself to have psychologically and culturally practiced a wrong or false identity during the period he was unaware of or unconscious to the more authentic African-centered identity. Similar to a recently recovered amnesiac who had assumed another identity for years, the newly Afrocentric person understood himself as becoming conscious of his true identity and, thus, was in the process of learning how to think and act in accordance with that identity. With an Afrocentric consciousness, there was a shift from the false identity to the authentic identity.

Those embracing Afrocentrism are not the only ones who understand themselves as becoming aware of their true identities and who consequently change their ethnic/racial labels and seek to learn their authentic cultures. In her ethnography, *Becoming Indian: The Struggle over Cherokee Identity in the Twenty-First Century* (2011), Circe Sturm examines the experiences of those who, as adults, shift their racial identities from white Americans to Native Americans. These are people who describe themselves as previously unaware of their indigenous heritage or who, for various reasons, had chosen not to acknowledge it. Many of Sturm's research participants explain that their ancestors deliberately hid their true identities as Native American in order to escape persecution and/or shame, as well as to access avenues of social mobility. Similarly, some members of First Afrikan discussed previous experiences of shame concerning blackness as well as suspicion that white culture endeavored to hide the true majesty of their African heritage from them.

Once they discover or acknowledge their Native ancestors, Sturm says that "many insist that their ancestors are literally embodied within them—as an essential, biogenetic, cultural and racial substance—and, if listened to, will guide them toward their true path and identity" (2011: 41). This idea that one shares not only genes but the same cultural and racial identity of her ancestors, no matter how many generations removed, and that there is an essential way of being and knowing that connects one to her ancestors is another concept shared by the members of First Afrikan and the "racial shifters," the term Sturm uses to identify her subjects. Attendant to the idea of an essentialized connection to African or Native American ancestors is the conviction that these identities trump or supplant previous understandings of the self. In other words, though a person may have both Native American and European ancestry, for the racial shifter, the indigenous ancestry eclipses the European ancestry. For the African American, in the Afrocentric context, the African is often privileged over the American.

Another similarity between members of First Afrikan and Sturm's racial shifters is the belief that becoming aware or conscious of one's authentic identity is not sufficient. A person must also learn the culture. As both groups act upon this belief, interesting questions are raised. For instance, whose culture is to be learned? Just as most black Americans are unaware of what part of Africa their ancestors hailed from or to which ethnic group they belonged, many racial shifters are making their best guesses at to their claimed ancestors' tribal affiliations. Most racial shifters do not have documented proof of their Native American ancestry and use family lore to retrace their roots. Consequently, both groups choose one of two routes: (a) cobbling together a pan-African or pan-Indian identity based on various beliefs and customs from a variety of ethnic groups, or (b) claiming one or two ethnic groups and seeking to learn their cultural ways.

As to the former choice, critics of Afrocentrism and Native American racial shifters point out that the selected cultural ways are often associated with an idealized and historical Africa or Native America where people lived in harmony with the earth, family dynamics flowed smoothly, and all shared a deep and primordial spirituality. Not only does this scenario simplify the histories and varieties of these cultures, it also ignores the ways in which contemporary African and indigenous peoples live.

As to the latter choice, many Native Americans take umbrage to racial shifters' efforts to acquire their culture. For instance, those racial shifters who have shifted to a Cherokee identity often request that documented Cherokee people instruct them on their language, religion, and other social practices. In addition, they may request participation in various cultural activities. Many documented Cherokee believe that Cherokeeness is an identity that must be lived and experienced from birth and not one that can be learned as an adult. Racial shifters are also suspected of desiring the privileges of an exotic identity without having to experience the burdens of a marginalized one. Furthermore, "there is a widespread concern that a significant number of race shifters are imitating, appropriating and sometimes even exploiting" Native American heritage as they seek a sense of cultural fulfillment and social belonging (Sturm 2011: 104). From the perspective of the Cherokee, racial shifters are white people who find white culture empty, do not have a strong attachment to any European ethnic culture, and do not feel that they belong to a sufficiently venerable social group. In Carmen's description of why she felt attracted to Afrocentrism, we see a similar dynamic when she said, "It seemed so often that, you know, us, black people, we just really just kind of did whatever. We never really had a way of life."

The Cherokee refer to racial shifters as "Wannabes," as in "want to be" Indian. Perhaps African peoples have a similar term for or concern about black Americans who, as adults, appropriate their religions, languages, names, dress, hairstyles, and foodways as they seek a more authentic and fulfilling cultural identity. In his study of African vendors of Afrocentric products in New York, Paul Stoller found that there was a certain irony to being "a real African in an African American economic niche that has constructed ideal Africans living in a largely imagined Africa" (2002: 82). For the most part, these vendors tap into the commodification of a monolithic and idealized Africa by positioning themselves as real Africans selling authentic African items. This positioning elides the issue that many items are just as likely produced in Asia or New Jersey and that those products from Africa are not identified with either a specific ethnic group or artist (Stoller 2002: 85). Although these African vendors take advantage of African American struggles with identity, there may nevertheless be discomfort with the collapse of a diversified Africa of multiple ethnicities into a one-size-fits-all African-ness and the subsequent cultural appropriation of such by others.

Furthermore, as identity is more than the practice of culture through language, religion, and dress, can one truly embody Africanness in America without the experience of living the identity in Africa with other Africans? In addition, African peoples may wonder why the Afrocentric are not satisfied with their blended African and American selves, especially considering the rich, varied, and meaningful ways in which black people have created and continue to create culture and identity in the United States.

Importantly, many, though not all, racial shifters and the Afrocentric believe that they have a valid claim to this cultural knowledge because of the shared ancestry. They do not see their lateness at coming to a Native-centered or African-centered identity as a barrier to claiming access to it. In fact, they believe they are experiencing a false self if they do not acknowledge and practice the identity. There is a difference between the two groups, however.

For racial shifters, claims to Native American identity may include feelings of entitlement to political privileges and economic resources as well as cultural practices. In addition, by shifting identity from white to Indian, one is moving from the group that oppressed Native Americans to claiming an oppressed identity. While there is possible cultural capital to claiming Africanness, there are not many economic or political benefits. Nor is there a history of black Americans oppressing Africans except, perhaps, in Liberia.

Another difference between Sturm's racial shifters and the members of First Afrikan is that the Afrocentric individuals are not changing their *racial* identity. Before and after understanding oneself as Afrocentric, the members of First Afrikan are black. Because Afrocentrism is not only about a relationship to Africa and Africanness but is also about negotiating blackness, the next chapter explores the theological teachings and the discourses concerning blackness as articulated by the leadership. In particular, it probes the relationships between African-ness and blackness as well as the ways in which blackness is and is not essentialized. Finally, the chapter considers the varied ways through which individual congregants define and understand their own blackness and that of others.

3

"Who I Am and Whose I Am"

Race and Religion

Existential Angst

I met with Hamida one morning for breakfast. Fifty-six years old, she is a tall, slender woman with high cheek bones and a quiet attractiveness. On this morning, she wore gold-wire-rimmed glasses and was dressed in a roomy black caftan emblazoned with a golden and swirling African design. As we spoke about First Afrikan's assertion that many Bible stories took place in Africa. Hamida explained,

> It's actually one of the most appealing things I found about the church. And I say that, because throughout the time I had spent in church as a young person, not once did it ever dawn on me that there was that possibility. I just took it at face value and, with all the images that were presented, that they were white. But when I think back, I realize that there might have been some part of me that rejected some of what we were being taught back then because I had never read the Bible from cover to cover. When it was pointed out that the Bible stories are in Africa, then it became so important to me to really be able to read the Bible and make

that connection. So now, I have no problem picking up the Bible and reading it.

A corollary of African-located Bible stories is the contention that several biblical figures were therefore black. In sermons and during Bible study classes, the church leaders devoted considerable time to drawing parallels between the physical and cultural similarities between biblical actors and African Americans. Through this Afrocentric reading of the Bible, the leadership hoped to instill not only pride but also a sense of spiritual specialness. A core message of the church was that people of African descent have a particular and special relationship to God and that, in order to truly understand themselves as African-centered people, members needed to be aware of and celebrate this connection. I asked Hamida about the connection between biblical and African American blackness.

"Is there a difference between black people in the Bible and black people today?"

"From what I know about the people in the Bible, I would say their Africanness was a way of life with them. For us now, it's not. That's the main difference. Nothing more comes to mind," she responded.

"What does it mean to be African?"

Hamida answered, "It's a tie, a connection that you have that goes all the way back to the very beginning. To have a strong sense of pride and know your origins. Knowing your origins, or if you don't know it, try to learn it and—and just being what it is that is inherent to you. Because I find that we have to suppress so much in order to conform. When we suppress what it is that we really are because of the societal pressures, then that's when you really realize how much of an African you are, because you are not really being yourself."

Hamida explained that she had joined First Afrikan Church because her true African self was nurtured there. She emphatically declared, "At that church, I know who I am and whose I am!"

"I know who I am and whose I am" is a phrase I was to repeatedly hear in the church. To me the phrase encapsulated the spirit and purpose of First Afrikan Church. First, the phrase raised the question "Who am I?" Of course, this is a question with which most humans grapple. For a member of First Afrikan, this question was often significantly contextualized by his struggle to understand himself in relationship to his African heritage. "Who am I?" led to the questions What does it mean to be a person of African descent in the United States? What does this Africanness mean in terms of my consciousness and in terms of my ethnic and racial identity? How should I perform my identity so that others will recognize and understand me as an African centered person?

By declaring, "I know whose I am," a member of First Afrikan stated both her relationship and her commitment to God. Embedded in this phrase is an understanding of the self as a "child of God," a familiar phrase in many African American churches. As a "child of God," one belongs to God much as a child belongs to a father. In belonging to God, the person has responsibilities to honor that kinship.

Therefore, the phrase, "I know who I am and whose I am" puts forth a construction of identity that emphasizes the relationship between God and Africanness. When a member of the church said, "I know who I am and whose I am," she was not just saying that she was of African descent and a child of God. Often, a member was also saying that as an African-descended person she had an especial responsibility to honor her relationship to God.

This especial responsibility was introduced and reinforced through the reading of the Bible as an African text. Members were taught to racially, ethnically, and spiritually identify with the characters of the Bible as fellow African-descended and black peoples. This chapter examines what the leaders of First Afrikan Church taught the members about "who they were and whose they were" with particular attention to the relationship between blackness and the Bible. In addition, I examine the contradictions between racial understandings of the self through an Afrocentric reading of the Bible and racial understandings of the self when considered in secular contexts. There is a significant shift in how blackness is defined and understood among the members when considered in everyday settings as compared to biblical contexts. In the secularized definitions of blackness, the church members' middle class status becomes particularly salient.

Preaching Freedom

In the orientation booklet for new members, Reverend Lomax explains the relationship between Afrocentrism and Christianity. He writes that Jesus is African, that the Bible is an authentic African document, and that, while the Bible is not telling a story exclusively to Black Americans, it is telling one *especially* for them:

> In it, we find the story of how a liberating God set an ethnically diverse African people free from the bondage of slavery. As a people enduring the North American Maafa, the Bible is a veritable road map to freedom. It not only reveals the path to freedom, but it assures us that the God of our ancestors is the God of freedom. Afrikan people have historically called God by many names. We have a multitude of ancestors standing at the ready to assist us in our struggle for liberation. As Afrocentric Christians however, we have decided to call our God, Yahweh, and our chief ancestor and savior, Jesus. (Lomax 2002: 5)

It is explained that *maafa* is a Kiswahili term. Kiswahili, also known as Swahili, is a Bantu language spoken by several ethnic groups, serves as a lingua franca in East Africa, and is the national language of five African countries. *Maafa* means "disaster" or "terrible occurrence" and is used to describe the more than five hundred years of exploitation of Africa through slavery, colonialism, and imperialism. "North American Maafa" refers to the experience of slavery in the United States and the continued racial oppression endured by African Americans.

Pastor Lomax explained that Christianity can serve as a bulwark against the oppressive condition of being a black person in the United States and that, eventually, God will provide African Americans liberation from their political, social, economic, and psychological bondage. In his explanation of Afrocentric Christianity, Reverend Lomax writes, "Though the context in which we live out our identity as Afrikans and as Christians is hostile, we are staying the course with the belief that liberation is soon to come, with the hope that a cultural and spiritual transformation is attainable, and with the determination to go to the cross if necessary" (2002: 20).

Also included in the new members' orientation material is a history of African American religion. In one section, it is explained that black religion has two motifs: the survival tradition and the liberation tradition:

> They represent two different kinds of religious sensibilities in the Black community. The survival tradition arose primarily among the slaves as an antidote to their expression of their dogged refusal to resign totally their humanity in the face of dehumanization. The Africans' use of conjuration, magic and voodoo and hoodoo, properly called vodun and obeah, was an attempt to survive the Christian brainwashing that accompanied their physical bondage. The liberation tradition grew out of the free Black community of the North. Its emphasis was on personal and social evaluation, moral behavior, and political liberty rather than sheer survival. (Lomax 2002: 39)

Black liberation theology is particularly important for contextualizing the discourse within First Afrikan Presbyterian Church. Black liberation theology emerged in the late 1960s as a "Christian movement of freedom for the transformation of personal and systemic power relations in American society at the point of racial difference" (Hopkins and Thomas 2001: 62). Within liberation theology, Jesus is interpreted as a political revolutionary who fought on the side of the oppressed and disenfranchised, and therefore his gospel has a "positive message about the negative racial conditions of Black people" (1998: 61). The theoretical father of black liberation theology is James H. Cone, who saw links between DuBois's double consciousness and black theology in that just as African Americans are both black and American they are both African and Christian:

> It was the African side of Black religion that helped African Americans to see beyond the White distortions of the gospel and to discover its true meaning as God's liberation of the oppressed from bondage. It was the Christian element in Black religion that helped African Americans to reorient their African past so that it would become more useful in the struggle to survive with dignity in a society that they did not make. (Cone 1992: 755).

Black liberation theologians maintain that biblical analysis and interpretation have been largely Eurocentric in that the academic field has
been dominated by European Americans and that they have not ade-
quately included the perspectives of people of color. While many black
theologians have sought to rectify this bias by attending to an analysis
that privileges the ways through which African Americans interpret the
Bible to provide spiritual relief from their circumstances, others have
sought to dismantle perceptions of the Bible as a European text. Of particular import is the argument that much of the Bible story takes place
in Africa and, consequently, that most biblical figures, most notably,
Jesus, are in fact African.

Cain Hope Felder, an Afrocentric theologian, takes exception to the
popular perception of Jesus as European and argues that there is "a critical need to examine not only how the fraudulent view emerged in Western history but also how the Bible specifically treats Africa, in general,
and Black people, in particular" (2003: 189). He believes that there has
been a deliberate attempt to obscure the role of Africa in biblical history. For example, although Egypt, Ethiopia, and other African countries
have prominent roles in the Bible, Felder alleges that "scarcely are such
ancient African locations portrayed fully in Bible maps in Europe and
especially the United States" (2003: 190). Felder also asserts that calling
Jesus "Semitic" is a deliberate evasion of his Africanness in that "Semitic"
refers not to a racial type but to a family of languages, including Hebrew
and Ethiopic and, furthermore, "that at the same time the European
academy coined the term Semitic, it also created the geographical location called the Middle East to avoid talking about Africa. Palestine has
always been where it is today, in Northeast Africa" (2003: 194).

For many Afrocentric liberation theologians, reclaiming the Africanness of biblical characters is key to a proper hermeneutic of the
scriptures. Some Afrocentric theologians such as Randall Bailey focus
on Africa as location and culture through a discussion of how it represented the ends of the Earth, military power, wealth, and wisdom to
ancient Israelites but avoid the issue of skin color (Brown 2004). For
others, the blackness of biblical characters is pivotal. Felder (2003)
notes, that while color prejudice and racial discrimination were absent
in biblical times, there is an occasional acknowledgement of black skin

color and that, when made, it is usually positive. While neither a theologian nor self-identified Afrocentric, the anthropologist St. Claire Drake also studied the issue of biblical blackness. He concurs with Felder that antiblack prejudice was absent during biblical times and even in medieval Western European Christendom, which venerated Black Madonnas and black Christian military heroes (Drake 1990: xviii). However, according to Drake, it was the white racism, which later developed, that denied the "Negro phenotype" of Egypt's political and spiritual leaders and denied that Egypt was periodically governed by "full blooded Black Africans" (1990: xvii).

Although there is some debate on the part of scholars about the ethnic and racial makeup of the Bible's characters and what relevance those identities have to contemporary racial and ethnic groups, at First Afrikan, there is no ambivalence. The church teaches that many of the central characters of the Bible phenotypically resembled African Americans and, because a considerable amount of the Bible story takes place within the African continent, that most biblical characters were to some extent culturally African. It is a core theme of the church that contemporary African Americans should identify both racially and culturally with the historical actors in the Bible.

Before looking more closely at the ways in which the blackness of biblical characters is constructed by the church, let us consider the varied meanings and definitions of blackness within the Unites States and in other parts of the world. This will provide a context to better understand the dynamics of constructions of blackness at First Afrikan.

Black Is, Black Ain't

"Blackness" is the quality or state of being black. But who is black? Is blackness determined by how one looks or by one's culture? Does a person choose to be black, or is blackness assigned by others? What difference do class, ethnicity, gender, or national identity make to the experience of blackness? When does blackness matter in an individual's life, and when does it not? Has there always been blackness? Is blackness a fixed essence, or does it evolve and change through space and time? These are questions with complicated answers.

Race

In order to comprehend blackness, we must first grapple with the even more complex concept of race. "Race," as we understand it today, was invented in the 1400s, when the desire for land, labor, and other natural resources propelled Europe's economic and political global expansion project and when Europeans needed to rationalize the campaign to dominate and exploit other societies. Bolstered by the era's scientific and religious thought, a belief in the God-given superiority of Europe was the foundation of racial ideology. The racial ideology included a classification of human groups as exclusive and discrete biological entities, arguments that the differences between groups were fixed and unalterable, and an inegalitarian ethos that required the ranking of these groups (Smedley 2011: 26). Also included in the emergent racial ideology were the concepts of "biomorality" and "essentialism." Biomoral thinking conflates the physical traits, temperament, and moral behavior of a racial group, while essentialism holds that members of a racial group share qualities that mark them as inherently different from members of other groups.

Racial categories were created to divide, exploit, and privilege different peoples. Racial ideology was employed to enculturate individuals to understand themselves as having race and to accept their place in the racial hierarchy. "The invention of race was a powerful transformation in the world's perception of human difference by imposing social meanings on physical variations among human groups that served as the basis for restructuring the whole society" (Smedley 2011: 22). Consequently, despite having no biological reality, race is nevertheless quite real as a social identity.

In sum, a race is a group distinct in phenotype and/or ancestry positioned in an unequal power relationship with other such groups. Racial ideology is used to assign and maintain differential levels of status and power within the larger society. Racial identity is a sense of collective identity based on notions of shared biology and ancestry, shared experiences of oppression or privilege, and belief in shared behaviors and other qualities that mark the group as inherently and immutably different from other groups.

Black people are one of the invented racial groups. African peoples of varied phenotypes, ancestries, ethnicities, religions, languages, and cultures were resituated on the African continent through European colonialism and dispersed throughout the New World through European slavery. The diverse collection of identities was reorganized into the singular collective identity of blackness through the power of racial ideology. As a racial concept, blackness depends upon shared ideas concerning phenotype, ancestry, status, culture, and other characteristics.

Blackness

Who is black? Black people are definitely associated with having brown skin and being of African descent. However, as a cultural construct, race is "dynamic, subject to oscillations in its expression and interpretation, from time to time intensified or contracted, sometimes modified or reinvented in response to changing circumstances" (Smedley 2011: 24). Consequently, blackness is an unstable concept, and who is black shifts through time and space. Blackness begs questions.

Are the indigenous populations of Africa black? The answer depends on who you ask. Most consider peoples from sub-Saharan Africa to be black, but North Africans are, at times, identified as ethnically Arab rather than racially black. One contingent defends the idea that North Africans are not black as they have a different racial and ethnic history. Another contingent considers the emphasis on ethnicity a problematic strategy to distance North Africa from blackness. The latter group contends that "North" and "sub-Saharan" are arbitrary categories that ignore that the Sahara cuts through some North African states. Furthermore, while many North Africans do have lighter brown skin that those in sub-Saharan Africa, there are indigenous darker-skinned groups in North Africa.

Are the descendants of enslaved sub-Saharan Africans in the Americas black? This question is also up for debate. The slave trade brought African peoples to Central America, and, for a considerable time, they constituted the majority of nonindigenous peoples. However, "while the majority of Central America's non-Indian population was no doubt of part-African descent, clearly that defined the lives of only some of the people and only at certain times" (Gudmundson and Wolfe 2010: 1). Central American states, seeking to be considered modern and part of the developing world, deemphasized their African roots and privileged their Spanish and indigenous ones. Consequently, "mestizo" or "mixed" is the racial identity of most Central Americans of African descent. A similar situation exists in South America. For example, Brazil received more enslaved Africans than any other country in the Americas and has the greatest concentration of people of African descent outside of Africa. Nevertheless, in the 2008 census, only 7 percent of people identified as black.

In contrast, in the United States, a person with any degree of African ancestry is considered black. The rule of hypodescent assigns children of a mixed racial union to the group of the lower status. In the United States, it is only applied to those of African descent, with the standard being also known as the "one-drop rule"—in that it only takes one drop of black blood to make you black. As with any rule, it can be broken. Historically, an individual who possessed phenotypic characteristics associated with whiteness or other racial groups could elect to "pass" as a member of that group. Importantly, the term "passing" suggested that the person did not cease to be black but rather denied or hid his blackness. In the contemporary context, one may choose to identify as biracial or multiracial. Nevertheless, for the most part, those with at least one black parent are considered to be black.

Can one be black and not be of African descent? Perhaps. Black wannabes or—the more controversial term—"wiggers" are white Americans who embrace African American culture and consider themselves to possess blackness in terms of behavior and consciousness, if not phenotype. Adopted by mostly poorer white Americans, "wannabehood provides a solution to the invisibility and cultural nothingness of whiteness" and is "a behavioral and identity alternative to the white trash label" (Wilkins 2008: 199). Although others consider their blackness inauthentic and suspect, for the wannabes, it is a meaningful and true aspect of themselves.

Therefore, as in these cases, to have blackness or not is dependent upon the dynamics of racial ascription and racial identification. "Racial ascription" is when others map race onto an individual so that a person in the Americas of partial African descent or a North African may be considered black by others even if they do not identify as black themselves. "Racial identification" refers to how the person understands herself and would provide blackness for a wannabe although others may refuse to identify her as such.

Putting aside the case of the wannabe for a moment, another question is, To what extent is blackness determined by skin color and other phenotypic characteristics? Quintessential blackness is imagined as brown skin, a prominent nose, full lips, and coily hair. However, reality is more complicated that the ideal. In Africa, people possess a wide range of skin colors, hair textures, and facial features. In the Americas, the sexual relationships between people of different African backgrounds as well as interracial relationships have resulted in even more varied phenotypic combinations.

Among people of African descent, skin color may range from coal to ivory; hair textures include short, tight curls as well as long, straight tresses; and any hair or eye color is possible. Within this wide range of phenotypic variation, all blackness is not equal. In the United States, "colorism" refers to intraracial prejudice based on skin color and usually, although not always, privileges lighter skin. As a consequence, black people may divide themselves into two groups. In black vernacular, one group is described as having fair skin, good hair, and pretty eyes, and the other group is described as having dark skin, nappy hair, and just brown eyes.

In Brazil, colorism includes those of other racial backgrounds, resulting in a pigmentocracy or society in which wealth and social status are determined by skin color. In fact, in Brazil, the term cor ("color") is more common than the term raca ("race"). "Color is often preferred because it captures the continuous aspects of Brazilian racial concepts in which groups shade into one another, whereas race is mostly understood to mean will power or desire" (Telles 2006: 79). Instead of the one-drop rule, Brazil employs blanquemiento, or an ethos that associates whiteness with progress and social mobility and darkness with primitiveness and social stagnation. The white-skinned people have the highest social status, followed by the brown-skinned, and last are the black-skinned. Brazilians navigate a folk racial taxonomy that includes some twenty-five or more options. Strategic combinations of skin color, eye color, hair color, hair texture, nose shape, and lip shape allow one to negotiate racial identity. For instance, a person with light skin and a generous nose and full lips associated with African descent may identify

as *sarara*, while a person with similar features and dark skin may identify as *preto*. Yet a person with dark skin but the more narrow nose and
thinner lips associated with European descent may identify as *cabo-
verde*. Furthermore, one's race may change depending upon context—at
work or home—and may not agree with how others have classified you.
For example, in public spaces, "the tendency is to minimize color differences, to appeal to a universalism," and so a person will avoid the
term *negro* ("African phenotype including very dark skin") and instead
use the term *escuro* ("lighter"). When describing loved ones, a person
"tends to give a few points on the chromatic scale—defining them as
lighter than they actually are," so that *moreno* ("mixed") is used in place
of *preto* ("very dark"; see Sansone 2003: 44).

African ancestry and brown skin are fundamental aspects of blackness. Yet blackness does not necessarily require either. In addition,
possessing both African ancestry and brown skin does not inevitably
determine one to be black. Culture is yet another slippery component
of blackness.

Culture and Status

"Black culture can be defined as the specific subculture of the people of
African origin," and it "supposes the transmission of specific cultural
patterns or principles from one generation to the next, within certain social groups, which might include a variety of phenotypic types
of people of mixed African descent" (Sansone 2003: 11). These specific cultural patterns and principles are largely understood to reflect
some degree of African influence. Although early theorists such as E.
Franklin Frazier (1957) argued that the processes of slavery robbed
African-descended peoples of most of their African heritage, it is now
commonly accepted that African American cultures, including those
of North, Central, and South America, retain significant African elements. These African retentions are evident in the religion, music,
language, foodways, and value systems. However, it should be noted
that the African peoples brought to the Americas were a heterogeneous collection of cultural groups who diffused customs and beliefs
between them, adapted those to the American contexts in which they
found themselves, borrowed cultural elements from other groups,

and created wholly new values and traditions—all of which eventually became the varied black cultures.

Consequently, theorists continue to debate the Africanness of the different black cultures. For instance, Afro-Bahians in Brazil are experiencing a process of re-Africanization, or deliberately identifying and engaging their African heritage. "This includes a conspicuous display of symbols associated with African roots in certain aspects of social life, particularly in leisure time and in local mass media" (Sansone 2003: 61). However, some contend that what is identified as African is not in fact very African. Rather, Brazilians are borrowing black cultural forms from the United States, cultural forms that are an amalgamation of different cultural influences, only some of which are African. The debate wrestles with how far removed from its original African inception a cultural element can be before it is no longer authentically African.

In sharp contrast to the Brazilian case, John L. Jackson found that some African Americans distance themselves from Africa and African peoples. His ethnography (2005) records a conversation about immigrant populations in Harlem during which one woman stated that "the worst thing is the Africans who come over here. You can't understand them." Her friend declared that most black people in Harlem are unconcerned about both Africa and African culture. "They don't know a thing about Africa except that it is far and got trees and animals." Jackson defines this perspective as post-Afrocentric blackness in which black identity does not "need Africa to authenticate and ground its legitimacy. It is a blackness that can invoke the African continent as an icon of heritage and history in one context while disavowing personal connections to other parts of the African diaspora in another" (Jackson 2005: 43).

Regardless of the degree of identification with Africa or the amount of authentic African elements contained within, the culture that black people in the United States share is the foundation of their identity as an ethnic group. However, black Americans do not share one ethnic identity. Rather, there are multiple ethnic identities differentiated by regionality, nationality, religion, generation, and other factors. In general, members of an ethnic group share beliefs, values, and customs, and they define themselves as different and special because of these cultural features. Markers of ethnicity may include a collective name, belief in common descent, a sense of solidarity, and association with specific territory; all of which are contained in blackness.

Blackness is frequently referred to as both a race and an ethnicity, with the two terms often conflated. This is because race and ethnicity have overlapping meanings and consequences as both are group identities based on shared descent, shared culture, and, often, shared physical characteristics. Furthermore, "ethnicity and race can be interrelated but distinct dimensions in the formation of individual and group identity, and, depending on context, one dimension may modify or take precedence over the other (Harrison 1995: 48).

The relationship between native-born African Americans and immigrant Caribbean Americans makes such interplay evident. Despite sharing a racial identity, Caribbean peoples of African descent who immigrate to the United States often insist that they are ethnically distinct from African Americans. On the one hand, "the immigrants see many differences in the home life of black Americans and West Indians, arguing that West Indians have stronger, more intact, families and stricter upbringing of children" (Waters 2001 65). West Indian immigrants also argue that they have a stronger work ethic and are less prone to criminal activity than native-born African Americans. For African Americans, on the other hand, the racialized aspects of blackness have priority over the ethnic ones, and they take umbrage when Caribbean Americans "distance themselves from American blacks and believe strongly that they did not want to be identified with American blacks or confused with them" (2001: 64). From the native black American perspective, their identity is largely defined "in terms of their opposition to the dominant group," and "a strong value is placed on solidarity and opposition to rules perceived as being against them" (2001: 64). Although, at times, distinguishing themselves from native African Americans in terms of culture, West Indians do concede that their common blackness is largely based on the shared experiences of oppression and sociopolitical marginalization.

As discussed earlier, racial ideology was developed to rationalize the exploitation of people of color and to maintain the social and political privileges of people of European descent. Blackness is consequently ineluctably linked to slavery, colonization, and marginalization. Furthermore, blackness "delineates a position in the social structure, one that variously informs or defines the life chances and experiences of people identified as black" (Hartigan 2010: 117). Although "racial meanings and hierarchies are unstable, this instability is constrained by poles of difference that have remained relatively constant: white supremacy and the black subordination that demarcates the social bottom" (Harrison 1995: 59). Who is considered black may shift from place to place, and ethnic differences may divide those so defined, yet blackness is consistently positioned as subordinate to whiteness. In sum, blackness contains within itself the effects of social marginalization, systems of exploitation, and other consequences of a subordinated status.

Collective Identity and Diaspora

One has blackness in the places where constructions of common ancestry and culture associated with Africa, phenotypic similarity related to brownness, and mutual experiences of subordination to whiteness have coalesced into a shared identity designated as "black." In addition, shared perspectives and notions of solidarity may result in a sense of collective identity. As with other aspects of blackness, this collective identity manifests in varied and fluid ways.

At times, collective identity through solidarity and shared perspectives may depend on notions of an African Diaspora. The African Diaspora refers to the forced scattering of African peoples throughout the world by slavery, imperialism, and migration. Diasporic identity contains within it a sense of shared history, ancestry, and culture, and it also suggests a shared allegiance and destiny. For some, mutual experiences of alienation created by the belief that they "are not and perhaps cannot be fully accepted by their host country" result in further feelings of solidarity (Clifford 1994: 304). Those engaged in diasporic consciousness see "the ancestral home as a place of eventual return, when the time is right," and "are committed to the maintenance and restoration of this homeland" (1994: 304).

Collective identity and Diaspora are dynamics in the relationship between African Americans and Ghanaians. The connection between the two groups began with the transatlantic slave trade, during which approximately five thousand enslaved Africans a year were transported from the coasts of Ghana to the United States. Later in the 1950s and 1960s, the connection between the two groups shifted from one based on slavery to one concerning emancipation as the two supported one another during their respective struggles for liberation—Ghana's fight for independence from colonial rule and African America's struggle for civil rights. The sense of solidarity between Ghana and African America was connected to the Pan-African movement.

Pan-Africanism seeks to economically and politically unify African-descended people into "one African community" and represents the aggregation of the historical, cultural, and philosophical legacies of Africans throughout history. During the twentieth century, the connection between Ghana and African America is evidenced by the Pan-Africanist and first president of independent Ghana, Kwame Nkrumah, and his participation in black political activity while studying in the United States, and by fellow Pan-Africanist and preeminent African American intellectual leader W. E. B. DuBois, who renounced his U. S. citizenship to become a citizen of Ghana.

However, despite the sense of a collective black identity based on a shared Pan-African history, in more recent times, the solidarity between the two groups has been somewhat disrupted. Ghanaians and African Americans have different understandings of their shared history of the transatlantic slave trade and, at times, different attitudes toward their shared blackness. These differences become evident when considering their perspectives on the Ghanaian slave dungeons, which held people before they were shipped to the Americas.

In the 1990s, many African Americans considered the slave dungeons along Ghana's coasts to be sacred places, as this was the final home for their ancestors before being transferred to plantations in the Americas. Each year hundreds visited the dungeons, such as Elmina Castle, hoping to pay homage to their ancestors and to make connections with their Ghanaian kin. Many of these African Americans arrived with the expectation that they shared an essential blackness with Ghanaians and that both groups would have similar feelings concerning the slave dungeons. Instead, what they encountered were Ghanaians who saw Elmina Castle as a museum representing both positive and negative moments in Ghana's history. Rather than preserve it as only a slave dungeon, they intended to paint it in bright colors and open a restaurant-bar (Bruner 1996). Furthermore, the Ghanaians did not necessarily recognize the African Americans as either kin or black, as they referred to them as *obruni*, "which means white man but is extended to Europeans, Americans and Asians regardless of skin color, so it means foreigner. This term was not extended to all non-Ghanaians of African descent as other Africans were called a term meaning stranger" (Bruner 1996: 295). In this case, whereas African Americans emphasized the shared racial identity of blackness, the Ghanaians instead emphasized the national identity and otherness of African Americans.

On the one hand, the African Diaspora can be a source of shared consciousness, as with Pan-Africanism, but, on the other hand, the African Diaspora can be a source of division. Throughout the African Diaspora are peoples of various nationalities as they resettled around the world, of various colors and ancestries as they mixed with other groups, and of various religions, languages, and other markers of cultural difference.

These dynamics of collective identity and difference between African Americans and Africans, the consistent experience of subordinate social status based on blackness, the question of how much African heritage is retained in African American culture, and the phenotypic criteria for blackness are issues at play in the construction of blackness at First Afrikan Church. During my fieldwork at First Afrikan, I found that the community employed the concept of blackness in the following four ways: as an ethnic identity, used somewhat interchangeably with Africanness, based on a aggregation of cultural beliefs and customs; as a racial identity privileging phenotypic characteristics such as brown skin, coily hair, and distinct facial features; as a sociopolitical identity typified by an experience of persecution and disenfranchisement; and as a collective identity, frequently constructed as an essentialized consciousness or a distinct way of comprehending and being in the world that inheres naturally in a person of African descent. A consideration of the discourse during sermons and Bible study classes reveals these dynamics.

Biblical Blackness

Let us begin with God. In his dissertation, Reverend Lomax wrote:

> The African God is Black. God is not Black because God is supposed to possess physical features like those of human beings. God is Black because God identifies with the oppressed Black African masses in

their struggle for freedom. From a spiritual perspective God's blackness means that God is the ground of being for all African people. Politically, the blackness of God means that God alone, not White racist oppressors, deserves the absolute obedience and veneration of African peoples (1995: 62).

In this argument, God's blackness is sociopolitical in that God is on the side of those who have been wronged through a denial of self-determination and self-sufficiency. Although in this instance blackness is synonymous with oppression, it is not only always conflated negatively with oppression. At times it is associated positively with originality. Citing anthropological evidence that humanity began in Africa, a discourse within First Afrikan is that God shares a special history with African peoples because, as the original people, they knew of God before all others. Following this line of reasoning, the church ideology asserts that Africans have the purest understanding of who and what God is and how to commune with the deity. This primal relationship with God is interwoven into the very ethnic identity of what it means to be African and manifests in the consciousness of black people.

It is important to note that Reverend Lomax does not say that God possesses the phenotypic characteristics associated with blackness. However, this is not the case when he writes about Jesus:

> Jesus the Christ was a Black African. Jesus was a Black African first, because he chose to be where Black Africans were, i.e., engaged in the struggle against the White Christ of the slaveocracy in North America. Second, Jesus was the Black African Christ because he was a descendent of Black African peoples. The blackness of the historical Jesus should not shock us. Even today, after centuries of intermingling with other peoples of the world, those people who are indigenous to the region of Palestine are dark skinned peoples. (1995: 67)

In this interpretation, Jesus's blackness is both sociopolitical and racial. In the first part of this excerpt, although referred to as African, this Jesus is one located within the North American continent. Employing a black liberation theological argument, Lomax refers to Jesus as one who fought on the side of abolition and civil liberty. In this case,

Jesus's blackness is like that of God's and based on social and political allegiances. However, in the second part of the excerpt, Jesus is racially black in that direct reference is made to his skin color. As proof of Jesus's blackness, I was to hear the argument in Bible study that, when escaping Herod as a child, Jesus was able to hide in Egypt because Hebrews and Egyptians were phenotypically similar in their brown skin. Corroborating evidence was to be found in the passage in Revelations that describes his hair as wool and his feet like brass as if burned in a fire. But the most compelling, and oft-cited, evidence offered is that much of Jesus's life took place in North Africa, which at First Afrikan is understood as a region of blackness.

In order to reinforce within the consciousnesses of the congregants the blackness of Jesus as well as other biblical figures, Lomax often took great care in his sermons to physically describe them. Jesus was usually depicted as a tall, brown-skinned man with long flowing dred locks and piercing black eyes as well as a nicely groomed beard of curly black hair. These physical descriptions of Jesus often included behavioral ones as well, with him being portrayed as one cool, laid-back, and compassionate brother. It was a recurring theme in Lomax's sermons that not only would Jesus be indistinguishable from contemporary African American men in terms of looks but also in terms of social temperament and cultural behaviors, thus implying both a biological and ethnic kinship based on a fundamental Africanness.

Reverend Coleman, too, took great pains to impress upon the congregants the blackness of biblical characters during Wednesday night Bible study. Having taken the introductory class the semester before, I was allowed to participate in Reverend Coleman's more advanced Hebrew studies course. Seated around folding tables arranged in a horseshoe configuration, there were some thirty of us students, each prepared for class with our Bible, paper and pen, class syllabus, and the numerous handouts on Hebrew and biblical history written by Reverend Doctor Coleman. Coleman was in the center of the horseshoe with his laptop and projector, which he used to display on the wall pictures of carvings, statues, and reliefs depicting Palestinian, Persian, Israeli, Assyrian, Sudanese, Egyptian, and other ancient peoples in battle.

As each slide came up, Reverend Coleman would explain why each group was fighting the other and whose war propaganda the carvings and statues were. His knowledge of not only biblical history but the cultural and linguistic history of each group was quite engrossing. But Coleman most captivated the class when discussing the pictures of Palestinian, Sudanese, and Egyptian peoples. Indicating a man in one of the carvings, he demanded of the class, "Who does that look like to you?" Putting his finger on the nose of one of the figures in the picture, Coleman then turned to Simon, a classmate, and proclaimed, "That is you brother!" He exhorted the class to see the physical resemblance between the ancient figures and ourselves as evidenced by their noses, curly and locked hair, and physiques. As he brought up closeups of the pictures, the entire class leaned forward and squinted their eyes to more clearly see what he declared was there. And even employing my most cynical objectivism, I had to admit that some of those noses looked quintessentially phenotypically black to me and that the hairstyles closely resembled kinks and locks. My classmates acknowledged with a collective "ah" that those certainly did look like black people to them, too.

Later, motioning toward a picture of a seventh- or eighth-century Assyrian sphinx, one student giddily observed that it still had its black nose and declared "that they didn't know about this one," referring to the widely held belief among the congregation that Napoleon destroyed the noses of the Egyptian sphinxes in order to hide their obvious Africanness. Reinforcing suspicions of deliberate attempts to obscure the Africanness of biblical figures, Coleman explained that the biblical city of Ninevah is now in present-day Iraq and that "Bush's war" could be destroying untold artifacts depicting images of African-looking people. These examples are part of a discourse within the church that those of European descent do not want those of African descent to know the truth about their relationship to the Bible in order to keep black people subordinated and, thus, that deliberate efforts are made to hide the truth through an appropriation of African history as European.

Around me, side conversations proliferated as people wondered at the shared blackness with biblical characters about which they had previously been ignorant and pondered the Eurocentric conspiracy to conceal this information from them. Why should this phenotypic resemblance to an ancient and foreign people mean so much to my classmates? What was so revelatory in a few depictions of generous noses and locked hair? For one, blackness as a racial identity assumed gravitas associated with noteworthy figures in the Bible. Second, it underscored the significance of an ethnic identity of both longevity and historical import, with the implicit assumption that if genetically related to these people, then contemporary African Americans must also be culturally related. And finally, it reinscribed a sociopolitical identity based on persecution in that attempts had been made to conceal the blackness of these biblical figures, thus misrepresenting not only their history but those of contemporary black Americans who shared it through racial and ethnic relatedness.

After the first two Wednesdays, the class shifted from looking for black people in the ancient carvings to a close reading of the book of Daniel. Reverend Coleman began the class by announcing, "When we say the Bible is an African book, that is what we mean. Not that you can *read* it as an African book but that these *are* African stories and prophecies." Here he was distinguishing between a black liberation approach, which encourages people to interpret the Bible from their own positionality as African-descended people, and an Afrocentric theology, which contends that those who wrote the Bible were in fact Africans and thus any reading of the Bible is to some degree African. More to the point, the stories in the Bible were about and for African peoples and their descendants. According to Coleman, one of the reasons that African Americans have had such an affinity for the text even from the times of enslavement is because they have an ancestral memory of it as it is part of their African legacy.

"Ancestral memory" is a phrase that Reverend Coleman frequently employed within class and during his sermons. It is an example of the fourth way that blackness is defined, as a consciousness. I gleaned that, for Reverend Coleman, all people of African descent share a consciousness that is particular to the culture and history of African peoples. This consciousness allows one to physically and metaphysically move in the world and to make moral and cultural decisions in singularly African ways. Apparently, some black people have repressed their ancestral memories more than others, but it inheres in each of them. More succinctly, Coleman defined ancestral memory "as the collective consciousness of a people." An example of this can be seen in linguistic practices.

For Coleman, the similarity between African and black American language ways is not just the retention of certain aspects of vocabulary and syntax but also in "the way people continue to say things. The way in which it [speech] is ritualized, the way phrases have a particular turn to them, have a particular rhythm to them. All these things are evidence for me of the ways language is retained through spirit or through energy."

What I was not clear on was how one came to acquire ancestral memories, as sometimes Coleman seemed to imply that they were passed culturally from generation to generation and at other times that they were genetically inherited in one's DNA. So I asked him and he explained:

> I'm talking about both. Because the [cultural] traditions are the idea that gods and goddesses are the supreme being, the idea of Orishas, ideas about rituals. Whatever it is that was a part of that West and Central African pantheon was in its own way, of course, created by the people and by their experience with the supernatural. At the same time, the experience of Maafa or crossing of the Middle Passage was transmitted not just through language but actually in the experience of the people that causes the DNA of a people to mutate or transform or adapt to the new environment and context. So these memories are a part of our pathos as well as a part of our joy and celebration. So all these components are what go into forming what I mean when I say ancestral memory. If a minister or a religious leader preaches or delivers a message in a very powerful way and the people in the congregation quote-unquote become possessed or become transformed or transported, these are not just accidental occurrences, these are part of African and African American cathartic and mystical encounters.

So for Coleman, ancestral memory or a collective consciousness is based upon African cultural beliefs and practices as well as on a metaphysical essence that evolves within and is transmitted through one's DNA. In the discourse at the church, it was conveyed that the more in touch with one's ancestral memory/collective consciousness, the more authentically African or black a person would think and behave. By returning to Hebrew class, one can see an example of this.

The book of Daniel is a compilation of stories about Hebrews who lived at the time of the Babylonian captivity. In part, it focuses on the tribulations of three Hebrew boys, Shadrach, Meshach, and Abednego, who refused to "eat the king's meat and to drink the king's wine" even when threatened by death for not doing so. The king recognized their faithfulness to their religion, spared their lives, and gave them high honors in his court. But in a reversal of fortunes, the mercurial King Nebuchadnezzar later threw the Hebrew boys into a fiery furnace when they refused to bow down to his statue. Happily and miraculously, Yahweh delivered them unscathed.

Part of the allure of this story for the class is that Coleman established earlier that Hebrew peoples were racially and ethnically African, as evidenced by the carved depictions and because Hebrew was a North African language. Another aspect is the sociopolitical identification with the captivity of the Hebrew boys in a foreign land, much like African Americans in the United States. However, what Coleman emphasized to the class was the consciousness of the Hebrew boys. "Even though they are in exile, they don't have exiled consciousnesses. Even though they are slaves, they do not have enslaved consciousnesses," he explained. The fact that the boys refused to change their Hebrew lifeways by eating and worshipping like the Babylonians was evidence of their Africanness. They remained true to their African culture and belief systems and, thus, were able to transcend the oppressive situation in which they found themselves. Similarly, it is those African Americans who have remained true to their fundamental Africanness who have also avoided exiled and enslaved consciousnesses and thus remained more authentically black.

* * *

Thus far, I have used "African" and "black" rather interchangeably, as that was how they were often employed in the discourses within the church. While, during my time at First Afrikan, I became persuaded of the Africanness of the Bible, I remained uncomfortable with referring to biblical characters as black. Although I have distinguished among four different ways that blackness was employed, the congregation made no overt distinction but rather utilized a biomoral approach. According to Eric Wolf, "biomoral thinking" is the conflation of physical traits, temperament, and political-moral behavior (1994: 4). In church discourses, both Africanness and blackness fluidly referred to phenotypic characteristics, ethnic behaviors, sociopolitical positionality, and collective consciousness and could refer to any configuration of these at any moment. Alluding to phenotypic characteristics as either African or black did not trouble me, but talking of the ethnic identity and sociopolitical experiences of both biblical Africans and contemporary African Americans as black did worry the anthropologist in me. This is because biblical Africans would have probably identified as distinct ethnic groups rather than through a shared identity based on skin color. Blackness, in contrast, is a contemporary identity based on phenotypic characteristics, a mélange of ethnic traits, and the experience of shared oppression. Although sharing with African Americans a glaringly similar predicament of being enslaved in a foreign land, possibly phenotypically similar to black Americans, especially considering the broad range that the term encompasses, and perhaps even culturally similar if one accepts the idea of core African traditions tying together North African and West African peoples, Shadrach, Meshach, and Abednego would have surely identified as Hebrews, not as black. But within the speech of my classmates, these shared ways of being made biblical characters and African Americans both black.

During my interview with Reverend Coleman, I explained my unease with the conflation of the Africanness and blackness in Bible class and asked if he considered it appropriate to refer to biblical characters as being black. His response to the issue of biblical blackness was that we cannot know how the characters of the Bible identified themselves because "the issue of ethnicity is not a biblical issue, it's a contemporary one." He allowed that blackness was an identity more appropriate to contemporary populations but that it was an important part of the class members' evolving consciousness to identify with the biblical figures as black, especially in terms of shared sociopolitical oppression, which was why he allowed the conflation of the terms. He also felt it important to counter images presented in popular culture that depicted biblical characters as white. Reverend Coleman was particularly incensed by *The Passion of the Christ,* a movie in theaters at the time: "It's ridiculous. *The Passion of the Christ* and Christ is speaking our language [Hebrew] but he is an Italian character. Come on!" Coleman explained that, in more advanced classes, he takes care to make distinctions between biblical Africanness and contemporary blackness. "So I tend to show that the characters are just as complex and multifaceted as we are today and that they also lived in a very different environment. I mean their experience as slaves was different from ours, although there are similarities."

Therefore, what Reverend Lomax and Reverend Coleman ultimately want the congregation to know is that many people of the Bible looked like them and that both groups were/are culturally African. Furthermore, it is through a reading of the Bible as an African text and how biblical Africans coped with oppression that African Americans will be able to spiritually and culturally escape the oppressive sociopolitical contexts in which they find themselves. Employing blackness as both an identity and heuristic device, the leadership seeks to reconfigure the consciousness of the membership to one that is truer to their ancestral legacy.

In Bible study classes and during interviews, the church members embraced the idea that they shared Africanness and blackness with some biblical figures. As Hamida put forth in the beginning of this chapter, and as was evidenced in the discussion of African culture in the previous chapter, members of the church were somewhat ambivalent as to how much Africanness they shared with African peoples, including biblical figures. When understood as a cultural identity, Africanness was often considered to inhere more authentically within people who were enculturated on the continent. Although many members suggested that essential aspects of African identity were naturally a part of them because of the shared ancestry, the efforts made to learn and practice African dress and language ways speak to an awareness that Africanness is to some degree learned.

As Africanness and blackness were both understood to have ethnic or cultural properties, and as the two terms were often used interchangeably, it could be argued that members were also ambivalent that they were as culturally black as biblical figures. As their ancestors were removed from Africa and because of assimilation into American culture, there was concern that contemporary African Americans had lost touch with the vital beliefs and practices and were no longer as culturally centered and proficient as they should be. Significantly, however, when blackness was constructed as a phenotypic and sociopolitical identity, congregants rather consistently professed a belief that both they and certain biblical figures, such as Jesus, were equally black. In addition, church members were convinced that they shared a black consciousness with their biblical African ancestors. Unlike culture, this black consciousness, reflective of the fundamental essence of who one truly is, cannot be learned, as it naturally inheres in one, although a person can be unaware of or disconnected from it.

As we shall see, for some members of First Afrikan, being disconnected and thus unaware of your authentic self may suggest that you are *less* black than others. Although persons may possess different degrees of blackness, most members insisted that all persons of African descent possessed some degree of blackness. According to all but a few of the congregants, no matter how consciously or culturally disconnected a person might be from his blackness, one could not completely lose the essential quality of being black.

Thus far, I have outlined some of the ways that blackness is employed within theological contexts as the congregants seek to better understand themselves spiritually and culturally through an identification with biblical characters. But what does blackness look like for the congregants when removed from the theological context? In the following sections, I examine how the members of First Afrikan understand the blackness of contemporary peoples of African descent. In particular, I more deeply consider notions of an essentialized blackness and the idea that there are degrees of blackness. First, though, we need to establish how the members of First Afrikan define blackness.

Blackness Defined

Frances Wilcox is a woman in her fifties with an open and friendly disposition. As we sat in her living room, brightly decorated in soft greens and pinks, she explained that blackness was for her a distinct way of being in the world:

> I feel as if it's how we move in the world. Um, it is the food, it is the music, it is the rhythm. It is the way we are loud. Usually, well mostly, but we *are* louder. It appears that we are louder, more jolly, and of course

this isn't in everyone. I'm thinking, we just have a way of being. I just, you know, I can't really expand any more on that. I think both. I think a lot of it is genes, and I think a lot of it is learned, but I think mostly it is there already. Some of us may choose to show it a little more than others. Some of us may try to suppress it and assimilate to another culture. But I think basically it is there.

Frances's description of blackness relies heavily on an essentialist notion of racial identity or, in other words, a notion that blackness naturally inheres in a person and influences his behavior. While she does talk about cultural behaviors such as food and music, the reference to loudness and jollity is spoken of as more of an innate quality. She forthrightly states that these behaviors have a genetic basis and that those black people who do not so obviously display these behaviors are suppressing their natural tendencies. At that same time, as evidenced by the caveats, she was aware that her definition was venturing into some murky waters with regard to problematic stereotypes of African Americans. Frances was attempting to articulate a sense that all black people share something vital. After all, Frances's investment in an Afrocentric identity rests upon the idea that, despite the experience of slavery and the centuries of absence from the Motherland, there was something that nonetheless tied her in fundamental and important ways to the place and ways of being.

A few of the other respondents dismissed blackness as not meaningful in terms of identity as it only indexed skin color, and not even accurately at that, since people are not actually black but different shades of brown. And yet these same respondents would refer to their blackness at different moments in the conversation, not as a skin color, but as a cultural identity. Despite having decided that they did not like the term "blackness" when discussing their identity, it was a difficult term to erase from their vocabulary.

Many of the respondents talked of blackness as a learned and cultural way of being. One of those is Jerome, a young man in his mid-twenties:

To me, blackness is like, is a style, you know what I'm saying? It's a way of life, it's a flavor, you know. Our way of talking, our way of moving, our way of dancing, you know. To me that's blackness, you know, that's black,

I guess. Race and genetics to me is Africa. Because to me, people in Africa didn't consider themselves black, they just were themselves, who they were, you know. And it wasn't until we saw white people that we started to call ourselves or think of blackness or we're black, you know what I mean. That was put on us by another race, and to me that's not good.

So within Jerome's definition, blackness is described in two different ways. The first is as a cultural identity, and the second is as a label imposed by Europeans. Of note, Jerome says that African people were not historically black, as blackness is a contemporary identity. However, in Bible study classes, Jerome referred to Jesus as black, suggesting a disconnect of some sort. Other members also made contradictory statements in their discussions of biblical and contemporary blackness. I suggest that, although phenotypic characteristics were emphasized in discussions of shared blackness with biblical figures, the real meaning of "blackness" in those contexts privileged consciousness and culture. In other words, the power of blackness was that it connected church members in terms of how they thought and behaved to their biblical ancestors. Moreover, as both biblical Africans and contemporary African Americans share a distinct way of comprehending and being in the world endowed to them through the essential nature of blackness, they shared the same identity or understanding of who they fundamentally were or were meant to be.

But, taken out of that theological context, blackness is employed in various ways—some of which privilege the sociopolitical dynamics of racial identity as well as the heterogeneous ways in which racial identity is constructed and experienced. For example, Carter's definition allowed for the idea that there are multiple ways to experience and express blackness as a result of the varied national and cultural settings in which African-descended people find themselves:

"So for me blackness is just all these black people coming from all over, bringing with them their own little piece of the pie, the quilt. So blackness is a mosaic of dress, music, speech patterns, accents, to some extent food, it's all of that. For me it's about these people that share this common attitude, but at the same time culturally, it's so diverse because we were scattered all over the place. And there are some commonalities no matter where we go, but at the same time a bit of flavor to wherever they took us. We somehow were able to get a hold of whatever they forced on us and made it our own. Whatever the ancestors left down to us over the years, we still maintain that, are able to add a little something to wherever we are."

When I asked Reverend Lomax to define blackness, he declined to do so and instead critiqued current definitions of blackness. First, he charged that groups other than black people have exercised far too much power in defining the identity and that black people should assume more control. He cautioned that as black people did so, they should keep in mind that, by its very nature, the meaning of blackness changes. For instance, Reverend Lomax believes that current articulations of blackness are rather stagnant and outdated—problematically wed to a specific point in history, the Civil Rights era, when the social and political context in which African Americans found and understood themselves was different than now. In order to construct definitions more attentive to current social and political dynamics, it was Lomax's opinion that African Americans must begin to create a more global sensibility of blackness:

> But who is redefining blackness, who says this is what blackness means in the twenty-first century? We are still stuck with that particular consciousness that came in the sixties. You are talking about a global type of government, you have people thinking globally, and we are still thinking about access in a particular place. I think that is backwards in some way. I think we have to think broader than that. You can see the African continent. You can see 80 million African-descended Brazilians, you can see 20 million Colombians, 279 thousand people in Amsterdam who are of African descent. You see it broadens us, and now you can think globally, too. There is a lot more available to you. It's about consciousness from my perspective. It's about how you see yourself in the world. One is thinking very parochially, and others have this global consciousness. Who do you think is going to win in that engagement?

Therefore, in Reverend Lomax's discussion, we see "blackness" described as fluid and subject to political and social dynamics. He also contends that blackness should be redefined in broader terms, allowing a more numerically, culturally, and politically strong basis from which to work. Added to the other definitions, there are several different perspectives on what blackness is. Some defined it as a natural way of being; others, as an inaccurate description of skin color. For some, it was a cultural identity, and, for others, an imposed label. It was also defined as fluid and having multiple manifestations as well as being diasporic with untapped social and political potential.

Carter's and Reverend Lomax's definitions put forth that blackness is heterogeneous and mutable. Yet, their definitions, as well as Frances's definition, also maintained that blackness has shared, quintessential characteristics that do not change. In fact, Reverend Lomax's ministry is largely based upon the idea that blackness has a consistent dynamic, an essence, that remains the same regardless of time or space as it is shared by ancient African peoples of the Bible and contemporary peoples of African descent. The final portion of this chapter considers the influence of essentialist thinking upon the construction of blackness by the congregants.

Shades of Blackness

> Ultimately, what makes a group a racial group is the belief that they are essentially different from another group. Racial essentialism means that groups are seen as possessing an essence—a natural, supernatural, or mystical characteristic—that makes them share a fundamental similarity with all members of the group and a fundamental difference from non-members. It does not change with time or social context." (Austin 2006: 12)

Throughout this chapter, we have seen examples of this approach to blackness. The Afrocentric reading of the Bible insisted upon an understanding that biblical Africans and contemporary African Americans were each culturally and spiritually shaped by the same black essence. This perspective asserted that conscious understanding of the self, perceptions and interpretations of reality, as well as the cultural behaviors and values of both groups reflected an immutable and timeless similarity that distinguished them from other groups and rendered them recognizable to one another. In this context, blackness is more than a genetic or cultural kinship; it is more than a sociopolitical identity. It is a fundamental and crucial way of being in the world that is transmitted and made manifest through this simultaneously natural and mystical essence.

Attendant to the doctrine of racial essentialism is the notion that all sharing a particular racial identity should also share a worldview and moral consciousness. In other words, they should have similar values and opinions. Consequently, embedded within essentialist thinking is the expectation that all black people should be ideologically aligned. When an individual black person veers from the group worldview or ideology, this person may be castigated or even ostracized. For example, an African American who prefers opera to jazz or the Republican Party to the Democratic Party is in danger of being told that she is a sellout or is acting white. In contrast to the Hebrew boys Shadrach, Meshach, and Abednego, such African Americans *are* "eating the king's meat and drinking the king's wine." In the contemporary context, this refers to African Americans who are considered to have too deeply assimilated into white culture.

As Afrocentrism takes as a central tenet that black people should embrace and practice African ways of being, knowing, and doing, how do the African-centered judge those black people who have different ideological allegiances? More specifically, is such a person considered less black? Does the assimilation of white culture or Eurocentric values lessen the quality of one's blackness? Finally, do the members of First Afrikan employ an exclusionary definition of blackness that invalidates the blackness of some? In order to address these questions, I asked participants if some people of African descent were more black than others and if some lacked blackness. In other words, is it possible that the black essence of some African Americans has been adulterated and compromised in some way?

When I posed the question of whether or not one could be too black or not black enough to Carter, he responded that it was an issue with which he had been grappling and about which he felt ambivalent. A part of him tended to categorize some people as less black than others. However, this was unsettling for him, as Carter was one who embraced diversity and intellectually refused the idea that there was a right or wrong way of being black. And yet there were those he considered outside the pale, so to speak. As he pondered his dilemma with me, he said that he was beginning to think that the problem lay in how blackness was defined. He charged that blackness was largely defined through negative and class-based criteria, rather than through positive and African-based criteria:

> The problem I'm having is that somehow we're defining blackness as mediocrity. It is less than excellence. So when somebody says she's not black, or he's not acting black, you're not dressing black, I'm having a problem. Because it's not that you're not conscious, which is how I see blackness. It's because you speak quote-unquote proper English, grammar structure, etc. etc. The blackness is you're not supposed to do well in school. That for me becomes a problem because I've always maintained that that's not my blackness. That's just an excuse because blackness to me says "excellence." You don't get jazz, you don't get creative cooking, you don't get hairstyles and all the things that we have given to the world with mediocrity. You get it out of excellence. Blackness for me has always been excellence, creativity, fortitude.

Many of the respondents echoed Carter's sentiments that blackness was often defined in class-based terms and associated with problematic behaviors stereotypically associated with poorer African Americans. For those who responded no, they did not consider some people less black than others, these respondents had typically experienced having their own blackness called into question. For example, Nina strongly rejected the idea that some people are more or less black, as she has been categorized on both ends of the spectrum:

> Looking at me, people will just say, I'm just too black, you know, just looking at me. And while talking to me on the phone, you would have no idea that I was black. So to me, I don't think there's any level of being black, it's just how you were raised. You're still black, you're still African American, and if you want to put me in a box and say, well, your level of blackness is here, mine is—I can't do that, no, I don't think so.

Derrick Saunders concurred that there are no degrees to blackness; rather, there are different ways of being black: "I think there are people who approach life in whatever way works for them. So I'm not going to say someone could be too black or not enough or whatever. I just think you are what you are," he explained. However, during the course of our conversation, it became clear that while there was no way to become less black, one could become dangerously tainted by whiteness. He explained that the older he became, the more effort he put into avoiding activities with white people for fear of becoming any more assimilated to European culture than he already is.

Several congregants asserted that there were many ways of being black and that when a person's blackness is called into question, it is frequently for not meeting class-based criteria. However, Beverly Rawlins was one of three persons who stated that some people were no longer black at all, having become too assimilated into white culture. According to Beverly, you could tell when someone had lost or never achieved blackness because of the way that they spoke, the clothes that they wore, and the activities in which they engaged. "Because of the way they were raised. They were raised in a predominantly white setting and they learned to think all white and never see anything from a black perspective. That's what I mean by not being black."

Beverly made certain that I understood that she did not exclude people from blackness because they were not speaking black English or listening to black music but, rather, because they were not being *African* enough. As an example, she recounted an encounter with her mechanic, who had a talent for carving walking sticks. When she pointed out to him that this was an African talent, he balked, saying that he was not an African, that he was black. By denying his Africanness and the manifestation of ancestral memory in his artistic abilities, the mechanic had failed her blackness test.

Frances Wilcox echoed the sentiments of Beverly that a denial of one's Africanness could manifest as a lack of blackness:

When I say not black enough I think of someone that doesn't want to identify with their African self. They may be okay with being, you know, black or African American, but not as far as to take it to that other level. I think that is where they may draw the line. So that's kind of where I'm coming from when I say someone is not black enough because I feel that they are not identifying with the true root. I feel that a lot of us are really brainwashed into the Western culture, and some of us go so far as to say we are not rooted from Africa. And I think like that when you are in a place like that, that you are really not getting it.

Thus far, most congregants believe that there are different ways of being black and that each is as valid as the other. However, even among those who do not wish to judge the blackness of others, as well as among those who are comfortable doing so, there is the belief that there are degrees to blackness. More specifically, those who do not acknowledge or are otherwise disconnected from their Africanness are less black than those who are more African centered. Another way in which a person's blackness could be called into question was if it were considered tainted by too much exposure to whiteness, especially the white power structure.

Condoleezza and Cynthia

During my fieldwork at the church, I noted that when discussions turned to politics the names of Condoleezza Rice and Cynthia McKinney were often mentioned. Not only was I intrigued by the prominence of two black women in discussions of American politics, I also found it interesting how each woman was constructed. On the one hand, Cynthia McKinney, a member of the House of Representatives, was characterized as a pugnacious defender of African Americans and a relentless critic of President George W. Bush. McKinney received national attention when she asked for a federal investigation into whether or not the Bush administration deliberately failed to prevent the catastrophic events of September 11. Secretary of State Rice, on the other hand, was the central figure defending the Bush administration during the federal 9/11 Commission hearings and emerged as an influential confidante of and advisor to President Bush. Whereas members of First Afrikan constructed McKinney as representing black interests, Rice was rendered as comfortably ensconced in the dominant white power structure.

Catherine McBride explained,

Cynthia hasn't lost sight of the needs of the future. And she's willing to step forward and take on whatever issue she has to take. If she feels like what she's doing is for the right reasons, she's going to go out; she's going to fight that battle; she's going to stand toe to toe. So she's real clear about what's important to her and what's important to the people. She's not lying because of her job or because of a situation, because of a position. And I don't see Condoleezza doing that. And I don't know what goes on in her head and what's she's doing.

It is important to Catherine that when McKinney speaks out, it is on behalf of people of African descent and that she speaks from a righteous stance. Catherine believes that, when one privileges the Christian ethic of defending the oppressed and the Afrocentric ethic of defending those of African descent, one has gotten it right and is doing right. In contrast, Catherine constructs Rice as less than righteous, even dishonest, and as more concerned with her own welfare than that of the people.

Felicia Prince also focused on the perception that Rice has placed her own welfare above the welfare of the group. In Felicia's opinion, the secretary of state became so assimilated into the dominant Eurocentric culture that she forgot the history of oppression that African Americans have endured in the United States. Therefore, for Felicia, Rice values her job as a proponent of American politics more than her cultural obligations to African American people:

> You know, some people take their jobs just very seriously, and I can't, personally I can't do that. I mean, I am who I am, and I take it with me no matter where I am. For her, she shuts it off, you know what I'm saying? It's very hard for a lot of us who have so-called arrived to their standards and have forgotten so much of what they have done to us. You know, people always say you should forget the past. We should never forget the past. We should learn from the past. We should not dwell on it, but we should never forget because as soon as you forget, that's how you get taken away, which I think she has gotten taken away. And I'm sure it's really hard to see, to know where she was as a child and what happened to her friends, her childhood friends and for her to get there. But I'm a conspiracy theory person, so you know, she was there for a reason, you know.

In the latter part of her response, Felicia suggests Rice has become alienated from her black cultural allegiances despite her childhood experiences. Rice was friends with Denise McNair, one of the girls killed in the bombing of the Sixteenth Street Baptist Church by white supremacists during the Civil Rights movement. Interestingly, Felicia believed that the experience must have had such a profound effect on Rice that eventually she will shift her allegiances back to the black community. Felicia said she considered Condoleezza Rice to be similar to the character from the *Spook Who Sat by the Door* (Greenlee 1969), which is about a man who only pretended to be a patriotic American in order to insinuate himself into the government. Once safely ensconced, he began a revolutionary movement for black liberation. I reminded Felicia that some black people had hoped the same thing about Clarence Thomas, but that it did not seem to be the case. But Felicia maintained faith in Rice's recovery.

Kendra Allen was less optimistic about such a recovery. Kendra believed that McKinney was more in touch with her blackness because, unlike Rice, she resisted the white power structure:

> Because Cynthia to me is pro-African versus Condoleezza. I see her [Rice] as a very brilliant young woman, but I see her as a puppet in that political environment. You know, somewhat of a token. Whereas Cynthia is not. Actually, she is a maverick. She is going to—she goes against the system. So I see her as a much better black person.

Consequently, it is evident that this particular Afrocentric group holds the belief that the less African centered one is, the more compromised his blackness is, and that assimilation into Eurocentric or white culture is a particular threat to one's blackness. Yet this same group also believes that there are multiple and different ways of being black and that, for the most part, when a person's blackness is questioned, it is on the basis of class-based stereotypes associated with blackness. At the same time, the membership believes that there is an immutable essence to blackness that connects contemporary peoples of African descent to biblical peoples of African descent. How are we to understand these conflicting beliefs?

Conclusion

In part, the conflicting constructions of blackness can be explained by the complicated history and nature of the identity. Blackness is employed in multiple ways as a consequence of the transatlantic slave trade, which necessitated the creation of the blackness concept and which dispersed peoples into varied and ever-evolving sociopolitical contexts. "Blackness" refers to racial identity based on phenotype, ethnic identity based on culture, sociopolitical identity based on status, and to an African Diasporic collective identity. Each of these axes of blackness have different meanings and consequences to different groups of people depending on their national identities, their social contexts, and their relationships with one another and other racial and ethnic groups.

In part, the conflicting constructions reflect the identity politics negotiated by many cultural groups—the tension between group identity and individuality. On the one hand, groups strive to maintain cohesion among members. Through boundary maintenance, groups define who they are by erecting and defending lines of demarcation between themselves and others. This is accomplished, in part, by determining what values and behaviors belong to the group. In this manner, members establish that they are all "playing the same game" (Barth 1969: 18). In addition, the collective identity within the cultural group is validated and reified through comparison to another. From the group perspective, we understand ourselves to be us because we are not them (Barth 1969: 27).

The boundaries between groups are policed through forms of etiquette and judgment about identity and difference. This is where racial essentialism comes into play. By marking those behaviors, values, and ways of being that ostensibly define the nature of all black people, the members of First Afrikan are able to establish criteria by which they determine membership inclusion and exclusion. Racial essentialism hinders assimilation into the larger dominant group and maintains group cohesion by questioning the blackness of those who do not conform to community norms. Therefore racial essentialism provides the African-centered community a powerful way to create a collective identity through shared values and behaviors.

On the other hand, members within a group may have perspectives and behaviors that do not conform to the collective identity. Unfortunately, the emphasis on conformity to an African-centered cultural code and the insistence that a timeless and immutable blackness is shared by all persons of African descent can result in the suppression of heterogeneity among members. At times, it problematically codes as invalid or corrupted the construction, experience, and expression of identity of individuals.

The tension between essentialist and heterogeneous constructions of blackness becomes apparent at First Afrikan when discourses of blackness in the theological context are compared to those in secular contexts. In nontheological contexts, the parameters of blackness become broader and more flexible, and blackness can manifest itself in a myriad of ways, each of them acceptable. The only caveat is that there must be an acknowledgment of the relationships between blackness and Africanness. While the congregants essentialized blackness in terms of believing that all black people share it, they were reluctant to define blackness in such a way that anyone of African descent would be excluded.

As middle class African Americans who have to some extent assimilated aspects of what they consider to be Eurocentric culture, the members of First Afrikan are reluctant to judge the blackness of others lest their own be judged. In addition, they recognize that not only class but also nation, region, gender, religion, and other factors can have an influence upon how blackness is constructed and expressed for any particular person of African descent. As with Carter's definition of blackness, many of the congregants are aware of and wrestle with the tension between heterogeneous constructions of blackness and essentialized constructions of blackness.

As their middle class status is such a key factor in the negotiation of blackness for this population, the next chapter will more closely consider the relationship between the two.

4

Ebony Affluence

Afrocentric Middle Classness

Scripture and Status

One Sunday, Reverend Lomax preached on the biblical character Zacchaeus and drew some compelling parallels between him and the membership of First Afrikan. The scripture for his sermon was taken from
Luke 19:1–10, which is about Zacchaeus, an avaricious tax collector
who, owing to his short stature, was obliged to climb a sycamore tree
in order to see Jesus as he passed through town. Jesus beckoned Zacchaeus from the tree and announced that he would dine at Zacchaeus's
home, much to the consternation of those from whom Zacchaeus had
collected taxes:

> With my mind's eye, I see Zacchaeus as a man with almond brown skin,
> bright smiling brown eyes, a sharp nose with mildly flaring nostrils.
> A white turban is wrapped perfectly around his head, and his brown
> ankle-length gown is covered by a burgundy and brown striped robe
> made of expensive Egyptian cotton. One huge golden ring encrusted
> with rubies rested comfortably on his right index finger. His hands

and fingernails betraying the fact that he was the consummate pencil pusher. Zacchaeus was a clean brother. He was sharp as a knife. Clean as the Board of Health. Why was this man who clearly had it going on, this man who was obviously well paid and well off, this man by all accounts a bona fide liability to his community—why was he chosen by Jesus as the man with whom he would stay? Well, if you want to know the truth about it, most of us here today have much in common with Zacchaeus. We, like Zacchaeus, are well fed, clean, and bejeweled. Now I know that we don't like to see ourselves as middle class or even as middle income people. We bristle at the notion of being labeled as middle class.

This portion of the sermon has several components of interest. First is the description of Zacchaeus as an African man and a person of middle class status. His middle classness is established by the clothing and jewelry as well as his bureaucratic position. Second is the assertion that his well-paid status suggested a traitorous relationship with his community; that he had been handsomely compensated for putting the needs of the establishment above his own people. Attendant to this dynamic is the implication that there is a tension between loyalty to the state and loyalty to one's cultural group. The final point of interest is, despite bristling at the notion, that members of First Afrikan are indeed themselves middle class.

This chapter will draw upon these points to elucidate class dynamics within First Afrikan Presbyterian Church: One, just as Reverend Lomax established Zacchaeus's status employing particular markers, the chapter discusses the ways in which the members of the church define middle class status. Two, it considers the middle class congregation's anxieties concerning both possible alienation from the less affluent black community and assimilation of white middle class cultural values. The chapter then probes the ways in which Afrocentric ideology both colludes and conflicts with middle class aspirations. Finally, it examines the intersections between middle class status, African American positionality, and loyalty to the state by parsing through the varied ways in which the members of First Afrikan understand their national identity.

A Middle Class Constituency

I first became intrigued with First Afrikan's notions of middle classness after reading the following excerpt from the church's website:

> First Afrikan Presbyterian Church is quickly approaching its tenth anniversary. God has richly blessed us. We have grown from 48 prospective members in April of 1993 to nearly 700 in January 2003. We have established ministries that effectively nurture our members spiritually, culturally, and intellectually. We remain steadfast in our commitment to be a holistic church, meeting the multifaceted needs of an emerging African American middle class constituency.

I was a bit taken aback that class would be featured so prominently in how a church identified itself, and, after noting the theme of class in some of the sermons, I began to wonder why this status was such a prominent feature for the leadership and if the membership concurred that First Afrikan was a middle class constituency. I asked Reverend Coleman why middle class status was included in the church's description of itself:

> I think it's more a recognition that most of the people who come to First Afrikan are coming from the middle class, and that it is our primary constituency. So it's described that way as an acknowledgment of who most often finds their way to First Afrikan and stays to participate in that ministry. So it's not saying this is the only class we want to work with, it's just most of us.

I did not survey the entire congregation to determine whether or not they considered themselves to be middle class, but I did ask the participants in my study. All but one defined the church as middle class. Beverly Rawlins said that the church was definitely not middle class. "Well, that's what they call it, but I don't think so," she said. She thinks that, as of late, more people of lower economic standing have joined the church. This was not necessarily a problem, she insisted, just something that she had noticed.

All of the participants, including Beverly, considered herself or himself to be middle class. I, too, categorize each of the participants as middle class. Many were not comfortable revealing their incomes, therefore I base this conclusion on their education, occupations, and neighborhoods. One of my respondents attended college for a year, four had associate degrees, three were in the process of completing their college degrees, four were pursuing graduate degrees, and four had graduate degrees. The remainder had completed four-year college programs. The participants included two nurses, one with a master's degree in psychiatry; two physical therapists; an office manager and service representative; three persons who owned businesses as a consultant, master tax preparer, and exterminator; four teachers and a former college dean; and others who held professional positions in the government or for corporations. I was able to visit the homes of all but seven of my respondents, and those houses I visited were located in what are considered the middle class subdivisions of Lithonia, Stone Mountain, and North Atlanta.

The criteria used by the participants to prove their own middle class status included income, education, occupation, and consumption patterns such as home ownership. Frances Wilcox based her class status on the combined salary of herself and her husband. Onaedo Odun considered herself middle class because that was how her natal family had always categorized themselves. "I've always considered myself [middle class]. I don't know. Just coming up that's what people always said we were. We're just middle class Negroes. Now, I'm talking about my family and what we said and what we did." The definition that her family used was having two working parents with the intention of sending all the children to college so that they would be able to do better than the parents. Valerie Owens considered herself middle class because she was in the process of buying her own home.

These parameters for defining middle class status, which include but do not depend upon income, correspond to the approach traditionally taken within black America. Historically, institutional racism prohibited even those African Americans with advanced degrees and professional occupations from earning the same income as their white counterparts. Unable to establish middle class status through significant economic advantage, traditionally the black community emphasized those behaviors associated with the middle class, such as a stable family, community involvement, church membership, and a respectable job. Whereas the American mainstream emphasizes income, African Americans tend to privilege educational attainment, occupational prestige, taste, and conspicuous consumption. "Class is viewed as a function of attitude, behavior, and personal character and is independent of power in the wider society. Views such as this illustrate how Black people validate themselves, in the face of racist assaults on their culture, by setting internal community standards for evaluating worth" (Vanneman 1987: 229).

An example of this is provided in Reuben May's ethnography *Talking at Trena's: Everyday Conversations at an African American Tavern*. Trena's Tavern is a place where middle class men with good jobs gather after work to relax and converse with one another. Importantly, "to the regulars, good jobs are not necessarily professional or white collar jobs but include blue collar jobs that pay sufficient wages for workers to care for their families, save a few dollars and enjoy the good life" (2001: 32). According to May, distinction was not made between white- and blue-collar jobs within the tavern because the patrons believed that racism and discrimination had negatively affected a person's chances of attaining the white-collar jobs. Nor was importance placed on salary. Rather, their middle class identity was based on shared values and ideals:

> They share the traditional middle class value of developing a career, rather than just holdin' onto a job. To them, education is so important that they express particular disappointment if their children have failed to take advantage of educational opportunity. In addition to beliefs about work and education, patrons share middle class expectations that leisure time should be spent traveling to exotic places and entertaining oneself with all of the latest mass consumer products such as big screen televisions, camcorders, DVD systems, computers and satellite dishes. (May 2001: 35)

In alignment with this dynamic, I found within First Afrikan Church that congregants forty and older were as reluctant to use income as the barometer of middle class status as the patrons of Trena's Tavern. However, members in their twenties and thirties were more forthright in making connections between income and class status. I hypothesize that the generational difference is a result of the barriers to equivalent middle class incomes with white Americans being lowered, although not completely eradicated, by Civil Rights and affirmative action legislation. Nevertheless, all age groups emphasized the role of profession, education, taste, values, and consumption patterns in their definitions of middle class status.

I met with Nina Kent and her husband Jerome, both in their mid-twenties, in their comfortable apartment in Northwest Atlanta. I asked what it meant to be middle class:

JEROME: Mmmm.
NINA: We talked about this before, didn't we?
JEROME: We did?
NINA: With Bill.
JEROME: I think so.
NINA: Well, maybe anywhere to $50,000?
JEROME: Middle class?
NINA: Well, no, to $75,000 a year?
JEROME: Okay.
NINA: Or thirty-five, I don't know, honestly. Anywhere from $75,000 to $100,000. No, 50,000 to 100,000.
JEROME: Yeah,
ME: So, fifty and below, is that working class?
NINA: Yes.
JEROME: Mmm, I'd go up a little lower than that, I'd say forty and below.
ME: Do you think that middle class is just about income or can it be about education and profession, tastes, lifestyle?
JEROME: Yeah, it has to do with all that. It's not just the money.
NINA: It's like when we hear people talk mostly, it's middle class is about money and how much they make.

Hadiya Hunter, a doctoral student in her early thirties, was to also offer an income-based definition of middle class. For her, the standard was between forty and ninety thousand dollars. However, she was to quickly add the caveat that middle class status was difficult to pinpoint for African Americans:

HADIYA: Well, in just some of my more recent readings, it's just with black people in the middle class, it's so much easier to, I guess, slip into a lower economic class just because there's not that generational wall to fall back on. As an example, I feel like I'm living okay, but if I were to lose my job or my financial aid or whatever, I'd be in big trouble. So I think a lot of people who consider themselves middle class, they're just a paycheck away. I think it may transcend income. But I think more so for black people it's easier economically to slip.

ME: So by "transcend," do you think middle class identity can also be about your profession, taste, and values?

HADIYA: I think it's a combination of all those. I mean I was just thinking as I was reading this summer, this book, *Black Picket Fences*, it's about the African American middle class. And I was thinking, if you lose your job, do you lose your middle class values? And, no, I don't think they just evaporate. And there are also people who have what are considered working class positions who have quote-unquote middle class values. So they're insuring that their children are going to the library, going to the museum, and all of those things. So while economically they may not be living a middle class lifestyle, they are making sure their children are exposed.

Hadiya was sensitive to the tenuous nature of middle class status for most African Americans who lack the buffer of wealth acquired over several generations by other racial groups. In part, because of this awareness, she allowed that black middle class identity incorporated a value system that could transcend economic barriers. This conception was also held by Catherine McBride, who, in her late forties, works as an administrator for a government agency.

Like most of the respondents older than forty, Catherine did not give an income level and resisted my attempts to cajole one from her. Rather, she emphasized certain behaviors, such as attending plays, as well as tastes, such as preferring nicer restaurants. Catherine did allow that most would consider her to be middle class but insisted that she does not think in terms of class. Instead, she classifies herself with those who have the same tastes and enjoy the same activities regardless of their incomes:

I don't normally think about put things in upper class, middle class. I do think it's a combination. I think there are just as many people that are quote-unquote, whatever you would call the range, not middle class but still want to go to plays, music, go to nice restaurants, and do those types of things. But if you don't have the money to do them, you find ways to be able to access it. If you couldn't afford to do it, then you become an usher and you can work in the theater and do those kinds of things. If you think in terms of middle class as people who wanted to own and acquire things and have the mindset to maintain them, I think that's part of it. I really don't think of that. I think in terms of the things I like to do. These are the things I like to go to. And so the people I associate with have to do those same things. And it doesn't—how much money someone makes, that doesn't matter. People like to do the same things. I really don't think in terms of middle class, upper class.

In his late forties, David Parson thought the church and its members were middle class because of their educational attainment. "I have no idea what the income level is, but from an educational standpoint, I would say yes because I think a lot of the people here have college degrees and have jobs that have titles. Some of them might have the money to fall in that group." Similarly, Anaya Duvant, fifty-five years old, said, "I feel that it's a middle class church because of the level of the teaching." For Anaya, the emphasis on learning within church programming signaled a middle class value system. She then added that the pastor's opinion has affected her own. "Because of that and because the pastor is usually talking about we're middle class. And just looking around at the people. I guess, I'm just assuming that most of the people are doing okay, and I don't know why I would just come up with that by looking at people."

For the most part, the members who used economic indices defined the parameters of middle class status as between $40,000 to $50,000 and up to $70,000 to $100,000 a year. Each person, however, indicated that income was not the only deciding factor and that profession, education, values, and lifestyles were just as important—for some, it was even more important. Having confirmed their understanding of themselves as middle class, I next consider how this status intersects with the congregants' constructions of blackness.

Colored Ambivalence

You had better come down Zacchaeus. Come down from the illusion that
has you thinking that you are better than the poor, sick and miserable
mass of humanity. Come down from the fantasy that has you believing
that your somebodyness is connected to your social and economic location in society. Come down from the fallacy that your perch on the tree
of systemic domination and oppression of the poor is safe and secure.
Come down from the myths that say you have pulled yourself up by your
own bootstraps. That you can do more from a position of corrupt privilege that you can from a condition of principled unity. Come down.

This excerpt from Lomax's sermon follows shortly after he suggests a
relationship between the nature of First Afrikan's middle classness
and that of Zacchaeus's middle classness. Here, the congregation has
become Zacchaeus, and Reverend Lomax exhorts his constituency to
be wary of believing themselves set apart from poorer members of the
black community. He tells them that inappropriate emphasis has been
placed on material acquisitions and that participating in the establishment's oppression of others, no matter how handsomely compensated,
is foolhardy and an act of betrayal to the community. Furthermore, the
hubris based on an assumption of individualistically acquired success
should be exchanged for principled action on behalf of all members of
the black community.

This idea of conflict between the class-based and race-based pri-
orities of the black middle class has a long-standing tradition within
academic discourses. In *Black Bourgeoisie*, E. Franklin Frazier (1957)
contended that the black middle class embraced the cultural practices
of the white upper classes and evinced disdain toward black folk culture. William Julius Wilson (1978) put forth that the social and political
interests of the black bourgeoisie and the black poor diverge as these
interests are more determined by economic factors than by racial factors. However, not all agree that class alienates the middle class from
the poor, as some theorists contend that the shared experience of racism trumps the alienating dynamic of class difference. Therefore, one
"can conclude that both classes believe that they are victimized by their
race and thus tend to have a more similar awareness of the meaning of

their race than the meaning of their class" (Durant and Sparrow 1997: 343).

Yet another perspective is that, rather than being completely class conscious or absolutely race conscious, middle class African Americans are instead somewhat ambivalent. In her book, *Blue Chip Black*, Karyn Lacy (2007) investigates the ways through which some African Americans negotiate this ambivalence. According to Lacy, middle class African Americans, on the one hand, strongly identify as and take pride in being middle class. They compare themselves to and expect the same privileges enjoyed by their middle class European American counterparts. Unfortunately, middle class African Americans must contend with stereotypes concerning blackness, specifically that most black people are working class or poor. For instance, a middle class black person in an expensive department store or neighborhood is likely to have others assume he cannot afford to be there based on the color of his skin. Lacy suggests that, as a result, many African Americans have learned to employ a public identity, or "strategic deployment of cultural capital, including language, mannerisms, clothing, and credentials," to convince others that they are legitimate members of the middle class (2007: 73).

On the other hand, while middle class African Americans want to be recognized as middle class and treated the same as their white middle class counterparts, they also take pride in their blackness and feel that "there is something inherently pleasurable about being black and maintaining a connection to other blacks" (2007: 152). Therefore, a middle class black person may employ race-based identities to signal that, although she may share a class identity with middle class white people, she does not share a cultural identity with them. One such race-based identity signal is the preference for black spaces, such as churches and neighborhoods.

However, according to Lacy, although middle class African Americans celebrate their connections to the black community, there is a limit to their identification with less-affluent black people. Exclusionary boundary work is employed to distinguish themselves from poorer African Americans. This exclusionary boundary work includes avoiding those things stereotypically associated with poorer blacks, such as certain styles of speech, clothing, and music. Significantly, the contradictions do not end there for middle class African Americans, as they may at times embrace the speech, clothing, and music associated with poorer African Americans in an attempt to access black cultural capital. The tastes, behaviors, and lifestyles associated with less-affluent African Americans are recognized by the larger society as racially and ethnically authentic, or, in other words, poorer African Americans are perceived as the bearers of true blackness.

Lacy has identified varied aspects of the conundrum in which middle class African Americans find themselves. They embrace middle class values, lifestyles, and privileges but eschew the ways in which these are simultaneously associated with whiteness. They embrace the joy and richness of black cultural life but work to avoid being mistaken for or, in fact, being too similar to poor black people. At the same time, middle class African Americans do not want to become so distinguishable from poorer African Americans that they are considered less authentically black. Public identities, race-based identities, exclusionary boundary work, and black cultural capital are just a few of the tools in what Lacy calls "the black middle class tool kit." This tool kit is necessary as middle class African Americans negotiate the pleasures, anxieties, and guilt associated with being black but not poor.

I contend that members of First Afrikan Church have added another tool to their black middle class tool kit—Afrocentrism. I suggest that, for many of the congregants, belonging to an Afrocentric church is, to some degree, an attempt to assuage the guilt and anxiety by, at times, emphasizing black identity over middle class status. However, the emphasis is not just on any black identity but on an authentic black *African* identity that can hold its own when compared to the black cultural capital associated with poorer African Americans.

Reverend Lomax's sermon about Zacchaeus tapped into worry on the part of the membership that their successful assimilation into middle class society could undermine their very blackness. A consistent discourse in the church is that middle classness is synonymous with whiteness and that middle class success is only achieved through an at least partial assimilation of white values and behaviors. For example, middle class status is often acquired by attending predominantly white colleges and universities and then working in predominantly white professional fields. Considered especially Eurocentric spaces, the fear is that one cannot be in those spaces without internalizing aspects of the culture. In addition, middle class cultural capital, or those behaviors and tastes that demonstrate middle class status, are strongly associated with whiteness. This includes standards of speech as well as tastes in music, clothing, and food. Consequently, if one is successful at being middle class—that is, white—then one is likely failing at being black.

However, belonging to an Afrocentric community provides reassurance to the individual and proof to others that one's blackness remains intact. Through participation in a community that values blackness and provides space in which to perform blackness, a middle class black person has some evidence that his assimilation into white culture is not complete. This is because Afrocentrism is understood as an antidote to Eurocentrism. As a member of an African-centered community, a person is deliberately learning and reinforcing the values and behaviors necessary to maintain a black identity. In addition, membership in an African-centered community signals that the person privileges black culture over white culture. This demonstration of loyalty in turn suggests that the person is resistant to being corrupted by "the system" and to possibly working against the interests of the black community. Finally, through socialization with other black people, the person is able to balance the effects of socialization with white people and is less likely to forget who "he really is."

Black middle class anxiety is not limited to fears of compromising one's blackness through assimilation of too much white culture. There is also apprehension about becoming alienated from black culture and thereby compromising one's blackness in that way. However, Afrocentric critiques of Eurocentrism and white racism help to offset these fears. These critiques emphasize the ways in which all black people are subject to experiences of racism thus making the argument that class-based privileges do not protect one from race-based oppression. In addition, by underscoring that the black middle class are particularly vulnerable to the deleterious effects of Eurocentric culture and must therefore even more deliberately value and practice authentic black cultural ways, the race-based bond is further cemented.

Consequently, among the varied outcomes achieved within the psyche of those belonging to the Afrocentric church, at least one is a sense of solidarity with less affluent members of the black community through a shared blackness based on shared experiences of racism and resistance to Eurocentrism.

However, the ability to share blackness with poorer black people is hindered because the popular definition of authentic blackness is not strongly associated with middle class African Americans. Within media representations as well as the commonsense notions of most Americans, black culture is associated with the behaviors and values of poor and working class African Americans. This is problematic in at least two ways. One, it suggests that there is one black culture rather than multiple manifestations of black culture that are nuanced by differences in region, religion, class, and other factors. Two, it stereotypes poor and working class black people as all thinking and behaving in the same ways. Nevertheless, within American culture, poorer black people are considered the real agents of authentic blackness, and middle class African Americans are often perceived by others, as well as by themselves, as less authentically black.

Afrocentrism provides a different way to see things. In the Afrocentric definition of authentic black culture, Africanness is considered a more genuine, original, and unadulterated exemplification of blackness than the class-based version. Hence, the Afrocentric definition of blackness, which privileges those behaviors associated with Africanness, provides a strong counterbalance to the popular construction of blackness, which privileges those behaviors stereotypically associated with the poor. In other words, through the practice of African cultural ways, the African-centered person is even *more authentically black* than the poor and working class person who is practicing a blend of African and American cultural ways.

With Afrocentrism added to the tool kit, the middle class church members are able to counter feelings of anxiety that they are becoming alienated from the community through over-identification with whites, feelings of guilt that they have abandoned their poorer skinfolk for the privileges of middle classness, and feelings of inadequacy that they are less authentically black.

Bourgeoisie Afrocentrique

Despite ameliorating troublesome feelings created by tensions between black identity and class identity, the Afrocentrically enhanced middle class tool kit does not completely resolve those tensions. Rather, at times, Afrocentrism complicates the ways in which people understand and engage middle class status. For example, at First Afrikan, there is a discourse that constructs the bourgeoisie and the Afrocentric as identities in conflict. Specifically, the conspicuous consumption and individualism associated with middle class identity was thought disruptive to the more communal and egalitarian ethos of Afrocentrism.

When asked if First Afrikan was a middle class church, Denise Payne said that she considered First Afrikan to be classless or without a class identity. "Because we don't—I don't think class—I don't really think we talk about class at First Afrikan. We're all just African." Carmen Sinclair explained that it was impossible to be sure how well members of the congregation were economically faring and that, in any case, such information was not important in the church:

> I think, you know, you can't really tell. And I say that because nobody really talks about what they do and how much money they make outside. So I don't know what everybody is unless it comes up. I mean, every now and then, like in time for Easter, they ask, you know, what our—we have to put on a paper what our job description was. But it's never asked and that was another thing that kind of drew me to the church, too. Because other churches, one of the first questions people always asked you was what do you do for a living. And I just always found that and "how much money do you make" to be very rude. And it's not because I make too little or too much, it's just not who the person is.

For both of these women, First Afrikan privileged other aspects of identity over class, and this was a significant reason each appreciated the church. Several members were critical of individuals who performed their class identity by talking about salary and consumption practices. There was the sensibility among the congregants that Eurocentric values privileged acquiring things and that materialism was a problematic and white-coded way of being. In fact, one member suggested that the church's Afrocentrism was compromised by its pre-occupation with middle class status. According to Valerie Owens, "It is very bougie—in my opinion. I'd say because, because . . . let me put it on the table. Because they could do a lot more if they weren't how they are. I have to say, they are too caught up in trying to be middle class. They don't do grassroots things." In her opinion, to be African centered meant that contributing to the community was more important than acquiring material possessions and performing one's class identity.

Although these responses contend that Afrocentrism and middle class status conflict with one another, Algernon Austin argues that the two, instead, have a symbiotic relationship: "Afrocentrism as a movement drew much of its strength from segments of the black middle class. The academics, intellectuals and educators who produced Afrocentric scholarship and ran Afrocentric educational initiatives were all middle class" (2006: 170). According to Austin, for Afrocentrism to evolve as it did, it required the black middle class who possessed the education and resources to learn African language and naming practices as well as to research African cultural history. It also required a black middle class with the financial means to purchase African clothing, art, and music and to travel to different countries in Africa. Furthermore, he contends that the black middle class had the financial means and leisure to nurture the cultural practices associated with Afrocentrism. For example, "Kwanzaa's increased popularity was the result of the actions of black middle class women" (Austin 2006: 170).

Austin provides two key reasons for why middle class African Americans, in particular, embraced Afrocentrism. First, it was an avenue to present themselves as culturally evolved as their white counterparts. Within the popular imagination, European or Western culture is constructed as the pinnacle of civilized achievement, while African culture tends to be constructed as less accomplished and, at times, even as uncivilized. Afrocentric ideology emphasizes and celebrates the accomplishments of African peoples and civilizations. Therefore, just as the white middle class could celebrate European history and culture, with Afrocentrism, the black middle class could laud African history and culture. Austin suggests that African-centered ideology was a means for the middle class "to prove that they were equal or superior to the white middle class by showing that they had equivalent or superior cultural capital" (2006: 171). This is definitely an ethos within First Afrikan Church as the members are very much invested in redeeming the reputation of African culture and demonstrating its parity, if not superiority, to European culture.

The second reason, according to Austin, is that middle class black Americans understood Afrocentrism as a mechanism to improve the social behavior and welfare of working class and poorer black Americans. The problems associated with the poor, such as low educational attainment and criminal behavior, were attributed to the poverty of black culture rather than to economic poverty or racially biased stereotypes. "Since having a bad culture was assumed to lead to poverty, it followed that having a good culture that instills the value of hard work will lead to success" (Austin 2006: 167). This reasoning concludes that what the black poor need in order to enrich their culture and thus their social welfare are better cultural values and practices. These could be acquired through a stronger knowledge of African history and culture. "It is assumed that if enough black Americans were to possess this African "ethnic" culture the success of black Americans would be assured" (Austin 2006: 168).

I did not hear discourses about rescuing less-affluent black people from cultural poverty in either the conversations with members or in the sermons of the preachers. The members did, however, discuss how they might use their middle class resources to uplift the poor and working class communities near the church. In an attempt to share their educational resources, in particular, First Afrikan established the Kilombo Pan-Afrikan Institute, which provides elementary education to low-income black children living in Lithonia. The director of the institute, Abeni Okonjo, explained, "Their curriculum is very African-centered, meaning that they are taught things from an African perspective." The mandate of the school is to enrich the children's education and family lives by instilling African-centered values and practices. Therefore, while First Afrikan does not validate Austin's claim that the Afrocentric middle class see the culture of poor black people as bad, they do substantiate his idea that the African-centered seek to use their resources to improve the social and cultural welfare of the poor.

In sum, the middle class Afrocentrics want to demonstrate their cultural equality to white middle class Americans as well as to lift up the working class and poor black communities. They simultaneously feel entitled to enjoy the benefits of middle class status alongside their white counterparts and fear that such enjoyment will alienate them from authentic black culture. Fundamentally, the Afrocentric middle class desire to fully enjoy the American dream with all of the benefits attendant to socioeconomic achievement *and* to participate in authentic black culture, albeit one infused with Africanness. Yet they fear that these desires are antithetical to one another. W. E. B. DuBois described the anxiety concerning this tension as "double consciousness."

Ever Feeling Two-ness

"Double consciousness" describes a phenomenon in which an individual's identity is divided into two separate, contradictory identities. For instance, in *The Souls of Black Folk*, DuBois wrote of the contradiction between black identity and American identity: "One ever feels his two-ness: an American, a Negro; two souls, two thoughts, two unreconciled strivings, two warring ideals in one dark body, whose dogged strength alone keeps it from being torn asunder" (DuBois 1903: 3). The members of First Afrikan Presbyterian Church experience a contradiction between their identities as middle class and their identities as black. As explained by Reverend Coleman,

> Being middle class means you have a series of complexities, contradictions going on that you're trying to resolve. I guess the plus side of being middle class in that broad sense is that we are well educated, we are fairly secure in our vocation, we have tremendous resources in terms of information about Africanness, to be sure, but also about the larger environment. The other side of that is that it brings contradictions that from time to time and can work against us because we still get caught up in ways of thinking and behaving that are not necessarily in the best interest of making ourselves or shaping ourselves as a new African. Because we're still bringing the ways of the master, we're bringing the language of the master, we're bringing the protocol of the master.

As middle class identity is associated with whiteness, the fear is that to fully embrace middle class status is to fully assimilate into white culture. If one were to fully assimilate into white culture, the accompanying worry is that one will be more loyal to the white community than to the black community. This brings us back to the sermon about Zacchaeus as a "man who clearly had it going on, this man who was obviously well paid and well off, this man by all accounts a bona fide liability to his community." It also connects to some of the rhetoric concerning Condoleezza Rice and the concern that unless one is diligent, the middle class African American may choose loyalty to whiteness, also understood at times as Americanness, over blackness. Within Afrocentric discourse, whiteness, Eurocentrism and Americanness are often conflated, as each are constructed as perspectives that privilege the customs, beliefs, and values of white people and marginalize the very same of black people.

In his 1897 essay, "The Conservation of the Races," DuBois approached the situation thusly: "Here then is the dilemma, and it is a puzzling one, I admit. No Negro who has given earnest thought to the situation of his people in America has failed, at some time in his life, to find himself at these cross-roads; has failed to ask himself at some time: What after all am I? Am I an American or am I a Negro?" (DuBois 1897: 12). Since then, African Americans of different class statuses and with different attitudes toward Afrocentrism have asked versions of this question. They have wondered if the Eurocentric cultural bias of the United States is such that black cultural values and practices are fated to be marginalized, disparaged, or ignored by the nation. Many African Americans have also pondered if the social, political, and economic privileging of whiteness fosters an environment in which black people are tempted to transfer loyalty from black America to white America. Black Nationalists are those who have concluded that Eurocentrism and white privilege do compromise black cultural identity and political solidarity, and thus, they advocate political and/or social autonomy for black people.

The core concepts of Black Nationalism "include support for African American autonomy and various degrees of cultural, social, economic and political separation from White America" (Dawson 2003: 22). Within Black Nationalist ideology is a desire to nurture black culture and to define "their identity by resistance to America and their determination to create a society based on their own African history and culture" (Cone 1992: 9). It is important to note that there is no one Black Nationalist approach, rather that African Americans have created varied Black Nationalist ideologies. For instance, Robinson points out that while Black Nationalist movements have consistently reacted to white racism, they have not unanimously rejected all things American and European. He has identified six different manifestations of Black Nationalism in American history. Religious nationalists combine Christian and Islamic beliefs with a desire for a separate state; revolutionary nationalists seek to topple capitalism; cultural nationalists hope to resist assimilation into Western modes of thought and practice; bourgeois nationalists combine mild cultural pluralism with a politics that expands opportunities in American society; and territorial nationalists demand separate territory (Robinson 2001). Many of the sermons and church activities of First Afrikan Church resonate with staunchly cultural Black Nationalist leanings, while the discourse of church members reveal both cultural and territorial expressions of Black Nationalism

One Nation under God?

During the summer of 2005, Black Nationalism was the theme of First Afrikan's three-week adult vacation Bible school. The summer program was called Camp Taifa; *taifa* means "nation" in Kiswahili. Camp pamphlets explained that First Afrikan was an institution committed to the liberation of all Afrikan people with a duty to teach the spiritual nature of Black Nationalism and to create a collective nationalist consciousness among the membership. The pamphlet guide read in part:

> Nationhood for Afrikan people is not a recent phenomenon, but a long standing aspiration of our collective reality. Our faith practice and our journey as Afrikan people has always been inter-related, never separate from each other. As Afrikan people, our goal is to exist on this earth so that the community is free to determine its own destiny and fulfill God's purpose for the life of the collective and the individual. Nationhood is a part of our creator's design for us. For Afrikans in America, nationalism is a critical tool of liberation. Nationalism has been projected as an essential element of any liberation movement (Nkrumah, Cabral, Nyerere, Garvey, Blyden, etc.) to restore Afrikan people from the Maafa.

Within the thematic design for the summer camp is the idea that, as Afrikan peoples, the members should practice self-determination. Components of this autonomy include having one's own land and independent institutions. During interviews, parishioners concurred that black people had an obligation to support the business ventures of other black people because circulating money within the community was a prerequisite to fiscal autonomy. It was largely agreed that money and control over its spending was necessary to the building of black institutions and that such institutions were required to create a truly African-centered culture. As its contribution to the larger Black Nationalist movement, First Afrikan had decided to concentrate on education. The leadership of the church placed considerable emphasis on education because they believed independent institutions of learning were required to properly inculcate the citizenry of the black nationhood.

Another example of the church's Black Nationalism is apparent in a series of sermons presented by Reverend Lomax on Melchizedek, a king and priest first mentioned in the book of Genesis. During these sermons, Reverend Lomax took great pains to explain how this biblical figure was in fact African and considered the "priest of humanity." Furthermore, Melchizedek's religious order included nation builders such as Abraham and King David. He told the congregation that Melchizedek should be considered a forefather of African Americans, in particular, and thus black Americans should understand themselves as direct descendants of this biblical lineage. He preached, "We are not the world's niggers, we are the priests. God intends us to serve this present age. We are priests in the order of Melchizedek. Know who you are and where you come from. You stand in the order of Melchizedek." As descendants of the African king and priest, he contended that African Americans are especially endowed as nation builders.

The crux of the message was, not that African Americans should build their own nation, but rather that they should see themselves as having agency in American nation building. The members were beseeched to understand themselves as being infused with the righteousness of Christianity and with the power that comes from African-ness and therefore as having vital roles to play in molding the United States into a more moral nation. According to Lomax, African Americans have a particular duty to improve the American situation, and this is a duty assigned by God and passed from African generation to generation through the lineage of Melchizedek.

During George W. Bush's presidency, Reverend Lomax preached numerous sermons lambasting Bush. He compared the Patriot Act and the War on Terror to "the repressive hate-filled government of Jesus's time." However, during several of these sermons, he asserted that, rather than separate themselves from the government, as African-centered Christians the congregation should actively participate in trying to change the government for the better. During the height of fears concerning post-9/11 terrorist attacks and growing intolerance for Islamic nationalism, Reverend Lomax put forth that it was the mission of black Christians "to be about love in the context of hate" and that "it is innately right that we love in the craziest of contexts." Reverend Lomax preached that, while he does not like George Bush, the call is not to like him but to love him, "to help him get in touch with his humanity. Our primary allegiance is not to Caesar, is not to the government, is not even to family and friends. It is to God." Therefore as African Christians, black Americans have a moral duty to be good Americans and to work to make the nation a more moral place.

Of note is that, although Reverend Lomax is critical of Eurocentrism, he does not advocate that African Americans should consider themselves in political opposition with European Americans. Rather, he offers an integrationist perspective that privileges the shared Americanness of both groups. Not only are African Americans integral members of the United States, even more explicit is the idea that African Americans need to take the moral lead in helping the United States achieve its more principled destiny as well.

James Cone explains that integrationists "believe that it is possible to achieve justice in the United States and to create wholesome relations with the White community. This optimism has been based upon the American Creed, the tradition of freedom and democracy as articulated in the Constitution and as supported by Biblical scriptures" (1992: 3). According to Cone, like Lomax, integrationists argue that "it is the task of African American leaders to prick the conscience of Whites"(1992: 4). Cone believes that African American preachers have been the most ardent proponents of this stance. Thus, we can understand Reverend Lomax's interpretation of the relationship between Melchizedek and

African Americans as being part of a larger tradition among black preachers. One notable preacher in this tradition is of course Martin Luther King, Jr., who fought for the dismantling of segregation and the full social, economic, and political inclusion of all people so that America could fulfill its promise as the beloved community.

Although in his discussion of Melchizedek, Reverend Lomax articulates a stance that situates African Americans as citizens with a moral obligation to heal their nation, at other times he articulated a definitively separatist position. Specifically, he asserted that despite the progress and accomplishments of black people within the United States, they were in neither the geographical nor cultural space where they belonged. On several occasions, Reverend Lomax insisted that African Americans were conscripted immigrants politically and spiritually languishing far from home:

> I am captivated by this notion of exile, I have to confess it to you today. Because that is where we all are. We are in exile. Life in America has become so ordinary to us that we forget we are behind enemy lines. We think we are doing well. We're alright because of what we are driving, the way we dress, and where we live. But the fact of the matter is that we are in exile. We are not in our homeland. We don't have access to our ancient cultures. Not really, not directly. We are not in the land where the stories are told. We are not in Mother Africa. We are in Ameri-KKK. And it is a land of exile, and you can tell it is exile if you would just look for a minute.

This language is, of course, reminiscent of Malcolm X's early black nationalism, which advocated social, political, and economic separation from European Americans. In theoretical analyses concerning King and Malcolm X, there is a tendency to create a dichotomy between them: the integrationist versus the separatist. However, as Cone notes, neither man was fully one thing or the other. Rather, their messages were more nuanced and overlapped in significant ways: "Of course, no Black thinker has been a pure integrationist or a pure nationalist, but rather all Black intellectuals have represented aspects of each, with emphasis moving in one direction or the other" (1992: 4). According to Cone, both Martin and Malcolm were actually somewhere betwixt and between the poles of integrationism and separatism.

In a given sermon, Reverend Lomax would preach about sociocultural exile in the United States *and* about the Americanness of black people with no apparent attempt to reconcile the seeming contradiction between the two. Both integration and separation are understood as coexisting within the lives of African Americans. Within the discourses of the church members are examples of an integrationist perspective as well as those of separatist perspectives. Of those toward the separatist end of the spectrum, most were cultural Black Nationalists. Similar to Camp Taifa and the sermon about Melchizedek, the point is not to create a separate political nation but, rather, to foster a cultural nationalism that privileges African-centered ways of being and thinking. However, at least one member of First Afrikan did advocate political and territorial separation from the United States.

Unreconciled Strivings
Proud and Patriotic

When I interviewed Beverly Rawlins, a former psychiatric nurse in the U.S. Army, we met in her home, a brick ranch-style house filled with pictures of her three sons, their children, and her friends. In her den, a Kwanzaa-inspired horn of plenty and African masks were displayed on a table, and she explained that she kept it out all year round, not just during Kwanzaa season. Along the other wall were memorabilia from her twenty-two years in the army. This included her medals, service pictures, and an American flag. She moved fluidly between fond memories of her time in the army to a proud recounting of her plentiful work on black causes that she had thrown herself into with gusto after separating from her husband, whom she described as an "assimilationist." She used this term to refer to his preoccupation with middle class status as well as his indifference to the cause of black empowerment. I asked Mrs. Rawlins what being an American meant to her:

> Being an American is that I have certain rights and privileges and also responsibilities. Responsibilities to, you know, to some of the principles. Even though I understand some of the principles didn't include

our people. But nevertheless it means standing up for your country and defending it. But not the wrong things. I couldn't join [the army] now, though. Then again, I could. Because that is how things change—by working within the system.

So while she acknowledged that the privileges of Americanness had not been extended to African Americans as they had European Americans, hence her participation in the Civil Rights movement, she did not see that as being in conflict with her identity as an American, as evidenced by her tenure in the army. Furthermore, she believed that it was by participating within the American system that African Americans would best be able to affect change. Others did not embrace as integrationist a perspective as she.

Somewhere in the Middle

Whereas Beverly felt there existed significant potential for the amelioration of oppression by taking advantage of one's rights and privileges as a citizen, most of my respondents were far more cynical. For the most part, they saw their Americanness as an identity that shaped who they were and granted certain social and economic privileges when compared to other nations. However, they also considered this identity an imposed one that they grudgingly tolerated and one from which they should try to escape if possible. Until escape was possible, they felt an obligation to protect select aspects of their American citizenship because previous generations of black people had fought so hard to acquire them for the group.

For example, Denise Payne felt that she had an obligation as an American citizen to vote, and she believed that African Americans should strive to be active citizens by running for office and attempting to affect change in the American political system. "Because our ancestors gave their life for it," she explained. "It's not that I necessarily believe in democracy, but I feel like [because] it's something that our ancestors fought for and died for, that we need to pursue it and make it better."

Yet, at the same time, she did not consider Americanness an important part of her identity because she felt that she was denied several privileges available to white Americans. She said that she was an American only insofar as it indicated her geographic location: "I was born here in America, and all my experiences come from me being an American, but they're so different from [the experiences] of other Americans. Sometimes I struggle with that, and I identify with it simply because of location and geography, just like I identify with being a resident of Lithonia, Georgia, but that's not solely who I am. It just identifies my location," she said.

Jacob Thorne also felt that black Americans had a duty to vote. But he did not construct voting as his obligation as an American citizen or as a tribute to the black Americans who had fought for the right. Rather, he considered voting an act of resistance against white racism: "Because it's a privilege and power to be able to vote. Because that was just something they just did not want us to do during that time or today. They don't want us to vote today." He also said that he did not consider being an American an important part of his identity but was more ambivalent as to whether or not he felt a strong commitment to the United States. He indicated that he was feeling less committed than usual because of the war in Iraq, with which he disagreed. "Like the war we're having right now, I don't feel that's in the best interest of the American people, especially black, because we're losing too many lives."

In consensus with other participants, Hadiya Hunter agreed that African Americans had a duty to vote because previous generations of African Americans had fought so valiantly to secure that right. And like many, she expressed an ambivalence about her identity as an American. On the one hand, Hadiya did not like the politics of the country, but, on the other hand, she confessed to enjoying the privileges of being an American in terms of the freedoms and a comfortable lifestyle. She was less ambivalent about her belief that African Americans would ever enjoy equal citizenship: "I envision, I guess maybe just forming our own nation. I don't think we can really ever be fully integrated into the American political system." She also feels she must participate as a citizen of the United States, not because she agrees with what it stands for, but because she feels more or less stuck: "I think they're the biggest terrorists, but it's almost like you're just kind of stuck in this land. Like, where would I go? I mean I said I would like to live in Africa, but could I really just pick up and be able to establish myself in a foreign land? I mean I guess people do it all the time but, you know."

Simon Vassey held the opinion that African Americans should not strive to be full members of the American political system: "No. Uh-uh. I just don't think that this American [system] is good for us. The American political system hasn't done anything for us. We need to have our own little political thing going on if we're going to have one." Although he did not like to admit it, Simon felt that being an American was an important part of his identity as it was the context in to which he had been enculturated. Like Hadiya, he would prefer to live elsewhere but resigned himself to this being where he was located and that Americanness shaped his identity.

Denise, Jacob, Hadiya, and Simon expressed double consciousness in that they felt that by immersion and participation in American culture, their identities were, in part, American. In addition, they felt that the American values of free speech and justice, as well as the civil liberties and social advantages enjoyed as a citizen, were positive and important to how they understood themselves. At the same time, each argued that this very Americanness was in direct conflict with another aspect of their identities, blackness. Specifically, each spoke of a sense of racialized political alienation and doubt that this alienation would ever be reconciled. While they imagined the solution would be to create a separate nation or leave, all four nonetheless participated in the political system with their vote. In partial response to this ambivalence, through their participation in an Afrocentric community, many of the participants considered themselves able to endure their marginality in the larger national community by creating an African-centered cultural nationalism in this smaller religious community.

A Separate Nation

Unlike the others, Uchenna Randolph intended to separate herself completely. Uchenna came to Atlanta in order to establish a branch of the New African People's Organization. Its Black Nationalist agenda is to claim the southern United States as a separate black nation. She explained that the organization started about twenty-five years ago and "was a way of creating a national organization for people who believed in independent nation-states, what we call an independent new Africa." Also included in the agenda of the organization is the idea that the remainder of the United States should become more attentive to the needs of all poor and oppressed people within its borders. Important to her understanding of an ideal nationhood was the concept of freedom that she considered unattainable as Americanness was currently constructed. Importantly, this freedom was not only intended for African Americans but to all cultural groups who embraced socialism.

I asked Uchenna if she in any way considered herself an American.

No. No, not at all. I don't even call myself American. I certainly live in America, I have America all up in me. Like I was telling you, it was a journey to become African-centered and to be whole. I have to battle some of the ideas and concepts I have as a product of being in America. Like Malcolm, I think we're victims of America. I know that a lot of black people consider themselves American; most of us, right? We've not even analyzed it, we just bought into it. But I think that will change as people learn more and grow more. I think America has blood on its hands. You know, the blood of the Native Americans, the blood of the Latinos, our blood, their own people they oppress. Karmically and spiritually, I don't think you can build something good out of something that began in evil and sin. So no, I'm not an American.

Uchenna was the only participant to definitively state that she did not consider herself an American. However, like the others, Uchenna did acknowledge that she was shaped by the cultural influences of Americanness. With the exception of Beverly and Jacob, the participants considered Americanness to be for the most part a burden that had been imposed upon them. Uchenna was the only one who took the more radical path of calling for an actual territorial withdrawal from the United States as well as for a socialist revolution. In contrast, while the others agreed with the idea that there was little hope of becoming fully integrated Americans, they stopped short of renouncing their American identity.

Conclusion

In her study, *Dreaming Blackness* (2009), Melayne Price considers the issue of Black Nationalism from the perspective of middle class African

Americans. Among middle class Black Nationalists, she identifies two types: those who embrace Black Nationalism and those who take a more moderate approach. Those who embrace Black Nationalism make blackness the primary lens through which they approach political loyalty as they believe white racism is the primary cause of the problems within the black community. By embracing Black Nationalism, they reject white norms and, instead, make African American identity central to definitions of themselves.

Moderate Black Nationalists struggle to balance racial loyalty with class differences. They acknowledge the impact of racism upon the black community but do not see that as the only problem. Higher incidents of crime, single parenthood, and other behaviors associated with less-affluent African Americans are blamed on the dysfunctional decision making of poor blacks rather t han on white racism. The moderate Black Nationalists walk "a tightrope between ideological communities. Whites have hurt them and members of their racial community, but they do not see all blacks as allies either" (Price 2009: 78). Although assigning different levels of blame to white racism, both of Price's types of Black Nationalists can be considered bourgeois nationalists, as neither act against the interests of their middle class status by advocating separatism.

According to Austin, the middle class gravitate toward the more integrationist bourgeois Black Nationalism because, while disaffected with Americanness, they are "not willing to make a more radical break from white America" (2006: 188). Instead, the middle class express "their frustration with white America through a type of cultural capital struggle with whites and not through ideas that would require disrupting their political and economic opportunities in American society" (Austin 2006: 188). In contrast, as the black lower classes have achieved less in socioeconomic terms and thus are less invested in a predominantly white America, he argues they are more prone to favor separatist versions of Black Nationalism.

In general, the membership of First Afrikan are bourgeois Black Nationalists. They have joined this Afrocentric congregation not only because they wish to celebrate their African heritage but also because they are sensitive to the ways in which blackness is problematized in the United States. As with Price's middle class group, many within First Afrikan privilege their racial identity and embrace Black Nationalism.

As with Austin's middle class Black Nationalism, the members of First Afrikan are, for the most part, proud of their middle class status and value the privileges associated with it. They view their middle class status as an avenue to improve their national status by creating independent institutions that serve the black community and by demonstrating their cultural parity with white Americans through veneration of their Africanness.

Nevertheless, the members are concerned that their enculturation into the middle class may lead to alienation from black culture. It is their hope that an African-centered identity will protect against such alienation but worry that the American part of their identity is antithetical to the very Afrocentrism they prize. Consequently, the membership experiences a two-ness as they negotiate the warring ideals of Americanness versus blackness as well as blackness versus middle classness.

Another arena in which the members of First Afrikan may experience a type of double consciousness is when negotiating the relationship between the tenor of black empowerment ideologies such as Afrocentrism, which tend to privilege masculinity, and the womanist theology espoused by the church leadership, which advocates gender equity. The relationship between Afrocentrism and Womanist theology is the subject of the next chapter.

5

Eve's Positionality

Afrocentric and Womanist Ideologies

Holy Gender Politics

I first became interested in the relationship between Afrocentrism and gendered dynamics at First Afrikan during one of my earliest visits. It was October 2003 and the pastor's birthday. During the meet-and-greet portion of the service, he stood at the front of the church shaking hands and hugging members of the congregation. Reverend Lomax was flanked by two tall women, each wearing a black pantsuit decorated with conch shells and with their locks arranged in elegant twists and loops upon their heads. The women stood on either side of the pastor, giving the distinct impression of being his woman warrior protectors. During the sermon, Lomax directly challenged the gender norms in the church and in the larger society. He told the men in the congregation, "You can be as macho as you want to be, but if you are filled with the Holy Spirit, you are filled with the her-ness of God. 'I am a man,' you say? Not unless you get in touch with the woman in you."

On another Sunday, Reverend Lomax preached about Jesus raising the widow's son from the dead. His larger theme was that the story is not so much about the miracle as it is that God cares for the last, the least, and the lowest. What I found interesting was his analysis of the parable as being about an anonymous woman in a patriarchal society having lost her only child, a male, which left her in dire straits and marginalized in a society that required women to be attached to and supported by males: "The story is not about the revived son but rather the widow whom the larger society might have ignored or turned against had she been forced to pursue less honorable ways of making a living."

Another interesting gender critique concerned King David and his relationship with his children. Reverend Lomax's larger message attended to the responsibility that parents have to discipline their children and the dangers of overindulging them. More intriguing, however, was his discussion of the patriarchal bias in how King David treated his son and daughter. David's son Amnon raped his virgin sister, Tamar. Apparently, David was angry about the crime but did not punish the son and even eventually forgave him. No biblical mention is made of David's behavior toward his daughter. In his sermon, Reverend Lomax denounced the men in Tamar's life who failed her: the father who permitted the situation, the brother who raped her, and the uncles and cousins who stood by and did nothing. He lamented that there was "no sense of compassion on the part of biblical scribes for the woman who was raped," and he pondered, "Why [is] the Bible silent about God's lack of intervention?" Reverend Lomax suggested that God did eventually act on the daughter's behalf and against David but that this was not recorded in the Bible because of patriarchal bias. In addition, he put forth that it was the sexism of the biblical scribes that rendered Tamar's voice silent and erased her fate from the passages.

In several of his sermons, Reverend Lomax asserted that the Bible was a patriarchal and sexist text. During my interviews, I asked members how they felt about this characterization of the Bible.

At sixty-six, Gloria Carnes is a brown-skinned woman with the soft roundness of a grandmother. I visited her home one afternoon and was invited to take a seat in the den, a warm room decorated with an eclectic blend of older women's bric-a-brac as well as African- and black-themed artwork. It was also filled with shelves of books and two couches amply supplied with pillows.

"Do you think that the Bible is a patriarchal or sexist book?" I asked.

"Yes, definitely," Mrs. Carnes replied. "I would try to read the Bible and just some of the things . . . " She paused for a moment. "The way women were treated in there, I always thought of as being second class citizens. You're being beneath man, subservient to. I just feel like that was the teaching, the way they presented it to me or the way I read it. It just didn't seem like we ever had any real anything when it came to the Bible. We were just servants or whatever."

I inquired, "Do you think that God has a feminine nature or that God can be referred to as she?"

"Yes, most definitely!"

"When did you come to believe that?"

"I always believed it. That's why I always stayed in trouble with Christianity. That's another one of those things where I say I'm beginning to better understand ancestral memory now. All those things that I always knew to be true but I couldn't understand why I was feeling this way, and no other people that I was around were feeling this way. Since I've been going to First Afrikan, I'm realizing that all the things that I've been really feeling are legitimate."

For Mrs. Carnes, despite what was presented to her in the Bible, she believed that women were equal to rather than subservient to men. She attributed this knowledge to her ancestral memories or a truth passed down through the generations from her African ancestors. First Afrikan Church was one of the few places she had this perspective affirmed.

However, not all members of First Afrikan agreed with Reverend Lomax and Mrs. Carnes.

I had become acquainted with Jacob Thorne at church, where he greeted visitors at the front door. Jacob is fifty-two years old, of average height, with a teddy bear rotundity and a bald head. When I asked him for an interview, he invited me to his home for breakfast. I enjoyed a meal of grits, eggs, and biscuits with special syrup from Maine.

"Do you agree that God has a feminine nature and can be referred to as 'She'?" I asked him.

"Yes," he responded. "That's true, because God is a spirit and we—nobody's never seen God, so he very well could be a woman or a man, who knows."

"Do you agree that the Bible is sexist and patriarchal?"

"No," was Jacob's response.

I was not sufficiently clever to get him to say anything more. So I tried another approach.

"True or false: Women should not do the same things as men. They are made, by nature, to function differently."

"Well, that's true. But women can do a lot of things men can do and a lot better than a man ever thought of doing," he responded.

"True of false: The male is the head of the household."

"Should be," was his succinct answer.

Within First Afrikan Church are some members who see the Bible as setting forth the appropriate power relationships between men and women and who have little to no qualm with its patriarchal tone. They sit side by side in the pews with those who are reading the Bible not only through an Afrocentric lens but through a feminist lens as well. This chapter is concerned with these gender dynamics.

Specifically, the chapter grapples with heterosexual gender politics. The church describes itself as a space open to persons of any sexual orientation, and participants assured me that lesbian and gay individuals and couples were welcome to join the congregation. However, during the period of my research, I was unable to recruit participants who identified themselves to me as gay, lesbian, or bisexual. This may be attributable to a weakness in my methodology or to the heterosexist bias associated with black churches, in general, and Afrocentric communities, in particular—or to a combination of both.

The first part of this chapter focuses on the womanist theological rhetoric of the leadership and its influence on the members' attitudes toward feminism and biblical gender dynamics. When the leadership employ womanist theology, they suspect that it is, at times, overshadowed by the church's black empowerment ideology and is, in some ways, in conflict with certain interpretations of Afrocentric thought. Therefore, the second part of this chapter considers the possible friction between black empowerment politics and feminist politics. This section also examines the church members' varied perspectives on gender politics between couples as informed by black empowerment and theological ideologies.

To Be Feminist, Christian, and Black

Before proceeding, I should define what is meant by the terms "feminism," "womanism," and "womanist theology." "Feminism" is an ideology and, at times, a social movement that advocates for political, economic, and social equity for women. Within some conceptions of feminism, woman are to be treated equally to or the same as men. In other interpretations, equity does not necessarily mean equal treatment as consideration is given to the social and physiological differences between women and men. Within either perspective, feminism seeks to liberate women from subordination and oppression based on their gendered and sexual identities. This includes the elimination of sexism, the unjust discrimination on the basis of sex or gender; androcentrism, the practice of privileging men or the masculine perspective in a society's worldview, culture, or history; and patriarchy, an ideology that justifies male dominance over women with regard to wealth, status, and power. It is important to note that "feminism" is a broad umbrella term for many different ideologies and movements that have varied perspectives on how to end gendered oppression. Within the United States, as in other places in the world, the agendas of feminists diverge depending on what aspect of identity is privileged.

For example, black feminism privileges the particular needs and experiences of African American women. Although African American women such as Sojourner Truth agitated against gendered oppression since the times of slavery, black feminism coalesced as a movement during the 1970s. In particular, its ideology spoke to the marginalization of women within black liberation organizations and the Civil Rights movement as well as to the marginalization of women of color in the women's movement and feminist organizations. As explained by the Combahee River Collective, an influential black feminist lesbian organization of the period, "Above all else, our politics initially sprang from the shared belief that Black women are inherently valuable, that our liberation is a necessity not as an adjunct to somebody else's but because of our need as human persons for autonomy" (1995: 231).

Tenets of black feminism are that black women share racial oppression with black men and that they share gender oppression with white women. Importantly, black feminism contends that black women experience the intersection of racism with sexism, as they cannot separate their blackness from their womanhood. Rather than privilege one dynamic of oppression over the other, black feminists put forth that the liberation of black women requires combating both forms of oppression simultaneously. Moreover, many black feminists argue that liberation for the black community cannot be fully realized without attending to sexism in tandem with racism and classism. Related to black feminism and a term, at times, used interchangeably is "womanism."

Coined by Alice Walker, "womanism" describes the experiences and perspectives of women of color. According to Walker's definition, a womanist is "a black feminist or feminist of color" and "a woman who loves other women, sexually and/or non-sexually." In addition the womanist "appreciates and prefers women's culture, women's emotional flexibility and women's strength" (1983: xi). Layli Phillips builds upon Walker's characterization and defines "womanism" as a perspective rooted in black women's experiences. However, she differentiates womanism not only from feminism but also from black feminism. Phillips contends that "unlike feminism, and despite its name, womanism does not emphasize or privilege gender or sexism; rather it elevates all sites and forms of oppression, whether they are based on social-address categories like gender, race or class, to a level of equal concern and action" (2006: xx). As concerns black feminism, she describes it as a sister to womanism and says that the two favor or resemble one another but are not the same. Specifically, Phillips argues that, as a black expression of feminism, black feminism is a perspective or social movement that privileges a gendered lens while womanism is "a social-change perspective that focuses on harmonizing and coordinating difference, ending all forms of oppression and dehumanization and promoting well-being and commonweal for all people, regardless of identity, social address or origins" (2006: xxxvi). Finally, Phillips emphasizes that an important and distinguishing characteristic of womanism is that it is spiritualized. "Spiritualized" means that it is informed by "spiritual beliefs and practices, rooted in the conviction that spiritual intercession and consideration of the transcendental or metaphysical dimension of life enhance and even undergird political action" (2006: xxvi).

Patricia Hill Collins does not fully agree with Phillips's more democratic definition of womanism in that Collins argues that race and gender are privileged over other aspects of identity. Referring to Alice Walker's metaphor that "womanist is to feminist as purple to lavender" and its implication that womanism is distinct and, in some ways, more profound than the feminism of white women, Collins argues that "this usage sits squarely in black nationalist traditions premised on the belief that blacks and whites cannot function as equals while inhabiting the same territory." Furthermore, because womanism censures whites axes of oppression, it "offers a vocabulary for addressing gender issues within African American communities" while simultaneously endorsing racial segregation. In other words, African American women are able to critique black male sexism without aligning with white women. Because of this basis of black racial solidarity, Collins contends that womanism provides an "avenue to foster stronger relationships between black women and black men" despite the critique of black male sexism (2006: 59).

Clenora Hudson-Weems also emphasizes the racial dimensions of womanism by marrying it to Afrocentrism. As the progenitor of "Africana womanism," Hudson-Weems describes it as "an ideology created and designed for all women of African descent" that "is grounded in African culture, and therefore, necessarily focuses on the unique experiences, struggles, needs and desires of Africana women" (2006: 48). Hudson-Weems distinguishes Africana womanism from Alice Walker's womanism in that the latter is more closely associated with feminism. Whereas Collins reads the purple as to lavender metaphor as a marker of cleavage between the two, Hudson-Weems reads it as a symbol of their affinity: "There is hardly any differentiation, only a slight shade of difference in color," she writes (2006: 48). She argues that feminism should be understood as an alien framework too closely associated with the Eurocentric experience and perspective. Furthermore, Africana women should be less concerned with gendered oppression and more concerned with racial oppression. "African people must eliminate racist influences in their lives first, with the realization that they can neither afford nor tolerate any form of female subjugation" (2006: 53). Hudson-Weems does not deny the sexism in the African American community but argues that it must be understood and dealt with differently than the sexism within the European American community. "While Africana women do, in fact, have some legitimate concerns regarding Africana men, these concerns must be addressed within the context of African culture" (2006: 51).

Similar to Africana womanism's distinction from feminism, womanist theology seeks to distinguish itself from feminist theology that is understood to privilege white women's perspectives. Womanist theology interrogates gendered oppression and contends that black theology has problematically privileged black men's perspectives. "Womanist theology challenges all oppressive forces impeding black women's struggle for survival and for the development of a positive, productive quality of life conducive to women's and the family's freedom and well-being" (Williams 1995: 67). The goals are not only to correct the biases of black theology and feminist theology but to also create a theology "about a holistic relation to the divine" as it argues "for positive sacred-human connections at the locations of gender, race, class, sexual orientation and to a certain degree, ecology" (Hopkins and Thomas 2001: 78). Furthermore, womanist theology is intended as "a sociopolitical analysis of wholeness" and seeks "to eliminate anything that prevents Black people from being whole, liberated people and from living as a whole, unified community" (Brown 2003: 297).

Part of the agenda of womanist theology is to reframe the ways in which biblical gender dynamics are understood. Womanist theologians contend that the patriarchal perspectives of biblical scribes and contemporary hermeneutics tend to marginalize, obscure, or erase the perspectives and contributions of women actors in the Bible. To correct this bias, womanist theologians work to reshape liturgical language by attending to the ways in which not only women but also people of color and the poor have been marginalized within biblical interpretations. The goal is not to rewrite the Bible but to read it in ways that acknowledge, redeem, and celebrate the roles, words, and deeds of marginalized groups, especially women, within biblical texts. "This means that womanist theology will consciously impact critically upon the foundations of liturgy, challenging the church to use just principles to select the sources that will shape the content of liturgy. The question must be asked: "How does this source portray blackness/darkness, women and economic justice for non-ruling classes of people?" (Williams 1993: 170).

This is of course not an exhaustive overview of any of the above ideologies; nevertheless, several aspects are pertinent to our discussion: (1) The pastoral leadership of the church tended to use the terms "womanism" and "womanist theology," not "feminism," "black feminism," or "Africana womanism." Therefore, I will favor the term "womanism" in my analysis. (2) Among the congregants, there were leanings both toward Africana womanism's assertion that racist oppression was more important than gendered oppression and black feminism's contention that true liberation for the African American community requires dismantling racism and sexism simultaneously. (3) Interpretations of biblical texts that moved women from the margins to the center were emotionally and psychologically affirming to several members of the congregation.

Sexists in Recovery

Throughout my time at the church, I heard both Reverend Lomax and Reverend Coleman refer to themselves as "sexists in recovery," and both were careful in their speech concerning gender, taking pains to incorporate feminist perspectives. Just as Reverend Lomax interwove feminist ideology into his sermons, in his book, *Tribal Talk: Black Theology, Hermeneutics and African/American Ways of Telling the Story* (1994), Reverend Coleman integrates a considerable amount of feminist theory and womanist theology. I asked both men about the womanist and feminist influences in their lives. Reverend Coleman explained how he had been introduced to womanist theology in graduate school:

> . . . because I was fortunate enough and blessed to be taught by womanist theologians, as far back as when I was a seminary student in the mid 1980's. Womanist theology is crucial because we came from Mother Africa. You've got to appreciate the African origin of all humanity, yes, but also the African *female* origin of all humanity. It's just that if we can't reconcile ourselves through that powerful presence and energy, we're going to be lost. So I've learned in my own life, in relation to my mother, in relation to my grandmother, very strong women in my life, that this is a power and presence that has to be appreciated. So to me, at this point in my life, it's a no-brainer.

Elder Itahari Toure, as the only woman in the leadership triumvirate, provides another crucial voice concerning womanist theology. When I asked Elder Toure if she was a womanist, she responded, "Absolutely!" She then proceeded to give me her definitions of womanism and womanist theology:

> It's kind of slipping away, but there are still remnants, but when women displayed this kind of authority, assertiveness and creativity—you were labeled to be womanist, as if it was something negative. So through the works of Alice Walker, she redefined them as positive attributes and that those were things we needed to celebrate, and it was patriarchy that was having us to think that these weren't attributes. Womanist theology takes that and says this attribute of who we are is God-given, it's God-defined. In fact, it is an aspect of the deity that we need to celebrate. It goes so far not just to recognize it, it also says there are particular systems that have been put in place to separate it from its divinity—patriarchy and racism.

It was clear from Elder Toure that she made meaningful connections between womanist ideology and a truly liberated and liberating theology. She also spoke of what it meant to work with two male leaders, who, although they had strong womanist principles, acknowledged that they were not immune to sexism:

> So as a womanist theologian, in this particular Afrocentric ministry, working with two recovering, as they have said, sexists, you can imagine the interactions we have in meetings sometimes. But as God would have it, it means my presence brings a balance. You have two very scholarly leaders here and I'm a scholar in my own right, but I bring a different energy. I bring a feminine energy that is authoritative—that says this is the way it's going to go. So Will [Coleman] calls me Missionary Itahari. On occasion, Pastor will say Mama Itahari.

As director of educational programming, she believed it incumbent upon her to make sure that women's issues and voices were included as the church decided on its educational agendas for the year. Elder Toure also found that she occasionally had to remind Lomax and Coleman that men were quite capable of assuming the secretarial, housekeeping, and child-care tasks that were necessary to run the church. Reverends Lomax's and Coleman's references to her as "Missionary" and "Mama" reflected both a certain amount of consternation for being taken to task, as well as a respectful acknowledgement of the status that she held within the group.

The status as the feminine authority in the church was quite important to Elder Toure, and she embraced the term "Mama," as to her it underscored the power and respect that women command in families:

> Everybody that I get to be in a relationship with, I get to be Mama, and I consider that just the ultimate blessing, the absolute ultimate blessing. I prayed many, many years ago that God would bless me to be a mother, and this was after I had my own children. I had always thought that as the mother of the church . . . I just feel that it is the ultimate testimony that you could have the freedom to express your love and it would be received. Because some people, you know, they've got a lot of love to give, and it's nobody receiving it. So I just think it's a tremendous blessing to be able to express love and to have it received.

From her vantage point as the mother of the church and as its educational director, I asked Elder Toure to speak to the strength of the womanist consciousness among the congregants. She said that it was in the beginning stages as people were comfortable with speech that referred to God as "She" but that, in her opinion, parishioners had a "ways to go" in terms of putting the theory into practice. "For example," she explained, "the Women's Ministry, for the past two celebrations, have read something from Renita Weem's work, but still it's in the affirming stage. It's in 'well, I'm so glad to know this and so glad that people care about this,' but it's not into the empowering 'act on it, don't let this be said about you or to you' stage."

Elder Toure felt that she must be patient concerning womanism as many of the congregants were still in the process of internalizing Afrocentrism, of rethinking their understanding of blackness. She was concerned that to press, at this point, for a reconceptualization of gender and gender practices might be too much for many of the members. She also felt that not enough safe spaces had been created in which women could experiment with what a womanist environment looked like. The church was providing that space to experiment with Afrocentrism, and she hoped to eventually create that space for womanism.

Upon speaking to congregants, I found evidence that the church is creating space for womanist speech, if not actions, at least insofar as concerns womanist theology. All of the people to whom I spoke agreed that God has a feminine nature and can be referred to as "She." However, while parishioners are apparently comfortable with the leadership doing so, only two of my participants, both women, themselves referred to God as "She" during our conversations. One of these women, Carmen Sinclair, said that she believed God to in fact be a woman, although she had some qualms about admitting this:

> I believe that God was a woman, and my mama's going to kill me for this. She thinks that's blasphemy, but I just—I think that God is a woman. [*Why?*] Because we were first in so many things having to do with creation—like Mother Earth. Like, I just think that's a part of the God within us to be able to give birth and to give life because that's what He did in the first place.

Evidence for a womanist theological perspective among the congregants could also be found in the almost unanimous agreement that the Bible is sexist and patriarchal. Jacob Thorne was the only person to disagree with this statement. For the remainder of the participants, hearing the womanist theology of Lomax, Coleman, and Toure was important to better articulating and coming to terms with their own critiques of the gender politics within the Bible. No one spoke to me of First Afrikan being the place where they were first introduced to the idea that the Bible is sexist; rather, they spoke of it being the place where their suspicions were affirmed and where they gained the language to talk about it.

The affirmation of women as equal players in biblical history was also a crucial component as to why Nina Kent gravitated toward First Afrikan. Even as a child, she had questioned the ways that women were presented in the Bible, being particularly upset with the absence of their voices and the practice of polygamy:

> You know what? Okay, this is why I always fought with this and I even asked my husband on how come. Does God think women are lesser

beings than men? I always used to think this when I was little, like why does—why is the woman always missing? Why does the man always have so many wives? Going to First Afrikan, we refer to women and men as both on the same level. God didn't make man better than a woman and we're not the subservient ones and the men don't have to be the head. We work together, we work together.

Felicia Prince enjoyed worship at First Afrikan because not only did Reverend Lomax make an effort to include the perspectives of women in his sermons but also that the value of women was highlighted in the rituals and practices of the church. For instance, some of the songs had been rewritten to refer to God as "She," the church's mission statement referred to women first, and Bible study classes provided background on the women actors in the text. Empowered by the rhetoric and practices of the church, after a discussion of the Holy Trinity at one of the church retreats, Felicia felt the need to insert femaleness into her understanding of it: "I always had a problem with being in church and the Father, the Son, and the Holy Ghost. My thing is the Holy Ghost is a woman. That was me, that's how I put her in, because you got to have a female in there. You got to have that—that balance in there."

Interestingly, although Felicia and the others have articulated quite womanist theological perspectives, none of them ever used the term "womanist" in our discussions. In fact, when I asked both women and men to define womanism or if they considered themselves womanist, most were unfamiliar with the term. Participants spoke of the value of women, of including women, of being prowoman, and of sexism and patriarchy, but only four respondents, two women and two men, used the terms "womanist" or "feminist." This is despite the fact that Reverends Lomax and Coleman as well as Elder Toure employed such vocabulary in their sermons and during Bible studies.

I posit three reasons for this. One is the general reluctance among women in the United States to label themselves as "feminist" as the term is associated with male bashing and lesbianism. Second is the particular reluctance of many African American women to so label themselves because it is believed that feminism is the project of white women while black women should privilege the fight against racism over that against sexism. Elder Toure provided the third reason. First Afrikan's leadership was not particularly adamant that congregants should think of themselves as learning womanist as well as Afrocentric theology because they feared that it would be too much change at one time. In addition, Elder Toure suspected that the Afrocentric environment itself made it difficult to create safe womanist spaces within the church.

What of Woman?

As a black empowerment movement, Afrocentrism has tended to privilege androcentric perspectives rather than treating women and men equitably. This tendency is well documented within the Civil Rights movement and among Black Nationalist organizations. As Afrocentric communities often imagine the idealized African family as a patriarchal one, Elder Toure cites this as another possible hindrance to creating a womanist environment. From her perspective, the cumulative impact of these androcentric and patriarchal tendencies limits the ways in which women understand themselves and the roles and behaviors they believe available to them. Elder Toure explained,

> One, the history of the movement in America for black people has been very sexist. So when you look back from the sixties and seventies where there were the Civil Rights or the Culture movements, women did not have a front row. As history came, we learned more and more about the role of women, but the brothers were supposed to be out there, we were supposed to be in the background. So first, it's difficult because even in a progressive mindset, women weren't supposed to be out front. Second, patriarchy is alive and well in many, many parts of Africa in the contemporary setting. Very few of us know about the Africa of antiquity where the feminine deity and feminine energy was more pronounced and put up front. We're now uncovering that. We understand, as we look back in antiquity, the role of the feminine energy even in some of the traditional religions. The deity that ushers in all the rest of the deities is a feminine energy. But we didn't know all that, so we got the king and the chief and this and that. We got all that information first because we were operating out of patriarchy.

The first part of Elder Toure's response refers to the marginalization of women in black empowerment movements. Black feminist literature frequently notes that, during the Civil Rights movement, most of the public leaders were men despite the considerable amount of ideological, grassroots, and administrative work accomplished by women. The feminist critique argues that this state of affairs was buoyed by the sexist and patriarchal tendencies that permeated black empowerment movements. During the Civil Rights movement, many contended that the success of black liberation movements in fact depended upon the privileging of men and masculinity.

In their book *Gender Talk* (2003), Johnnetta Cole and Beverly Guy-Sheftall identify specific dynamics of this debate. One, they note that black empowerment movements often equated the status of black men with the status of the group. In part, this reflected the androcentric nature of society, in general, and, in part, it reflected a racial argument concerning male oppression. "It was widely accepted that racism had emasculated Black men, prevented their legitimate claims to manhood, and compelled them to demand their rightful place as men (even patriarchs) in a white male-dominated society that had rendered them powerless," Cole and Guy-Sheftall explain (2003: 82). Part of this androcentric argument was the insistence that racism more profoundly affected black men, and because of their pivotal role in the black community, the empowerment movement should privilege their needs. Consequently, black women should support black men in the effort to redeem their masculinity in the public realm as leaders of the movement and in the private sphere as the heads of the household.

Concomitant to this stance was the mandate that black women should eschew feminism as it was considered in collusion with racism against black manhood. Antifeminist rhetoric contended that "Black women, more privileged by the racial and social order because they are less threatening, are powerful matriarchs who need to step back and support Black men's long overdue quest for manhood. In other words, racism privileges Black women and situates Black men at the bottom of the heap, reversing the natural order of things with respect to manhood and womanhood" (Cole and Guy-Sheftall 2003: 83). Furthermore, because racism had robbed black men of any meaningful social power, the argument followed that they were not in the position to oppress others, even black women.

In fact, some argued that the women were more likely oppressing the men through the emasculating nature of black matriarchy.
The argument that a woman as a head of household is problematic
was thrust into the mainstream consciousness in 1965, when Patrick
Moynihan identified the matriarchal dynamic as a key contributor to
black poverty and familial dissolution. Within some black empowerment organizations it was asserted that African American women
had assumed inappropriate amounts of power and authority within
black families as they were able to attain educational and employment
opportunities not available to black men because of the gendered racism of U.S. society. Consequently, black men were displaced from
their rightful roles as primary breadwinners and, as evidenced by sin-
gle-mother homes, were increasingly absent from black households
altogether. It was argued that without male role models but with models of female dominance, black male children were reared in emasculating environments.

As black women were imagined as the power brokers and oppressors within the African American community, feminism was viewed as
more applicable to white communities than black ones. This argument
ignored the ways in which sexism intersected with racism and classism
in the lives of African American women as well as the many ways in
which women were oppressed and abused by African American men, in
particular. Nevertheless, many men within black empowerment communities believed themselves the more vulnerable party and attacked
from two fronts—the oppressive nature of racism and the misapplied
critique of feminism.

Black women were "admonished to choose between loyalty to the
race and their own liberation agendas" (Cole and Guy-Sheftall 2003:
94). It was argued that racism was the urgent matter for the African
American community. Therefore, similar to Africana womanism, the
antifeminist argument contended that the perspectives and needs of
black womanhood were less urgent and could be dealt with at a later
time. In the meantime, black women were to concentrate on supporting
black men in the fight against racism and the gendered oppression that
black men suffered.

Kimberly Springer suggests that it was the reaction to these androcentric and patriarchal arguments that motivated black women to more

deeply develop black feminist thought and to more actively participate in the larger feminist movement: "Individual black women recognized male chauvinism and the devaluation of women's leadership capabilities in the civil rights movement," and they "reached out to one another to confirm that they were not alone in seeing disparities between the rhetoric of the civil rights movement and the treatment of women within that same movement" (Springer 2005: 45). However, more than thirty years after the apex of the Civil Rights and feminist movements, Elder Toure alleged that the antifeminist rhetoric in black empowerment movements such as Afrocentrism continue to frustrate efforts to create a sustainable womanist environment at First Afrikan. Therefore, in my interviews with church members, I queried the participants about a central tenet of the antifeminist argument.

Equality of Oppression

I asked church members if they believe black men are more oppressed than black women. Frances, a married woman in her late forties, believed that historically black men have suffered from racism more than black women. However, she added that the scales of suffering were balanced because black women endured abuse from black men who projected onto women their anger concerning racist mistreatment:

> I'm coming from the standpoint historically. Women could always find work, be it that we may have been working in the white woman's kitchen or suckling her child or whatever. But we were able to be self-sustaining in the fact that we could [work]. I think the black male was deliberately torn down because I think the oppressor was more afraid of the male than the female. I feel that, on the other hand, because of all of that within our own community, men have been so enraged with being displaced in that way, that a lot of times we [women] have suffered. Do you want to know about the present day? I feel that even today we're probably more educated, we live longer. So I still think probably because of that historical presence that we still have all that baggage to correct. The two genders have to figure out how we're going to reconcile that.

Most respondents said that men and women have it equally hard in the United States, albeit in different ways. As explained by Catherine, "I think we each have our own particular battles that we have to deal with. In some instances, yes, it's a lot harder for a black male, but in some situations it is very hard for a female. It just depends." However, Jerome suggested that black women may in fact suffer more than men because of the double burden of racism and sexism:

> I think the struggle is pretty much hard for both. I will say this, black women may have it—they may have it harder for this reason: they're black and they're women at the same time. And in society, those are two strikes. You know, I'm still male so I only have one strike against me, you know. So, in that respect, sometimes a black woman can have it harder. But then of course society really does put the weight on black men very hard, very hard; so, I could say it evens out. It's equal.

Asmina agreed that both men and women suffer different types of oppression, but she added that it was unhealthy for the black community to continue to be preoccupied with which gender has suffered the most:

> I think that discussion which has historically been on our plates forever is kind of unhealthy. I think we should bottle it collectively. There's different levels of oppression, and we both suffer from them. I think society is very frightened of the black man, and they attack the black man. And I think the black woman suffers from not only oppression from the general society but even from her man. So to say one is less oppressed than the other, I don't think it's healthy for us to do that. They're both different. It's kind of comparing cancer to diabetes. They're both going to kill you if you don't treat them. So yes, they are different, but one being worse than the other, I don't believe that.

In sum, the participants believed that men and women were both oppressed by gendered versions of racism. At least one participant thought the gendered racism visited upon men was greater but that he in turn oppressed black women with sexism. Another participant put forth that the intersection of racism and sexism was more oppressive for women.

For the most part, the tenet that black men's oppression is more substantial than black women's apparently has little purchase within the community. As the members believed that both women and men were subject to racial and gendered oppression, I probed their ideas concerning feminism.

Feminism

I employed the term "feminism" instead of "womanism" because it was a more recognizable term to the congregation. One third of the women that I questioned agreed with the statement that feminism was for white women and that black women should concentrate on black empowerment. For example, Hadiya said, "Personally yes, I agree. For me, personally, I think that it's more important to focus on the entire black race. I think feminism maybe has its place; but I think as a whole, we just have to work on the entire community."

Felicia, who earlier described how she amended the Holy Trinity to include a female entity, outright rejected feminism as black male bashing. She described it as

> going against everything, male, just everything [about] men—well, I'm not going to say everything. They go right on and they bash a lot of things that men [do]—so I'm not a male basher. Yeah, I mean you don't bash one another; you don't bash men to better yourself. That's how I feel, you know, it's like I don't.

However, Catherine took exception to the categorization of feminism as being about power struggles with men, black or white:

> See for me, when I think of feminism, for me as a black woman, it's about empowerment. It's not about having a war with men. You know, that's not what it's about. It's about empowerment. Being able to stand up for yourself. Being able to understand when you have to be strong, but [that] you don't have to be all the time. Being real clear about yourself. What are those things in life that you are willing to put up with and not.

Denise thought that feminism was particularly helpful to black women.

I do feel like during the feminist movement, that there was some progress for black women during that time. A lot of, like some of the abor-
tion issues were at the top of their game during that time and, of course,
women were coming out then politically. So during that time, it was
easier for a black woman to navigate politically during that time. And it
helped us, I think, as a family, because it allowed us to get some progress.
And it allowed us to have a voice within [the black community], so I
think in that way it helped.

Although Denise believed that feminism was beneficial to black
women, she did not employ the term "black feminism." When she later
commented that feminism did not deal with the totality of the black
female experience or with the experience of being a Christian woman,
I realized that she was unfamiliar with both black feminism and
womanism. In contrast, Asmina told me that she preferred the term
"womanism."

Asmina felt that "womanism" better captured the relationship
between racism and sexism than did "feminism," which tends to be
more closely associated with white womanhood. In Asmina's construction of womanist ideology, she privileged her identity as an African-centered person, although what she described was not Africana
womanism:

I am a New African Womanist. I wouldn't mind being called a feminist.
White women have nothing on us in terms of fighting for the rights of
women. Mary Chad and Ida B. Wells and Mary Church Terrell, they had
women's clubs over 130-something years ago, where they were fighting for
the rights of women. So no, that does not belong to white women. Human
rights are a human issue, and we deserve to be free as Africans and as
women. To fight just for black people means that we're still in bondage
as females, and we definitely suffer from such oppression. You have some
feminists who are bourgeois feminists, and they want to have equal rights
with their men, but they're not trying to fight the rigid gender roles or the
way society is. They're not really truly trying to fight patriarchy, they're
not really trying to fight imperialism, they just want a piece of the pie. But
I believe that there are revolutionary feminists who want to see a new day.
So I have no problems with the word "feminism." We use "New African

Womanism" just because we think it's more palatable to our people. But I don't have any problems with the word "feminism."

Like Asmina, two thirds of the women acknowledged that they held feminist perspectives. Nevertheless, most were reluctant to label themselves as feminists. The reluctance was largely because they associated the term "feminism" with white women and because they were unfamiliar with the terms "black feminism" and "womanism." Interestingly, only women voiced any opposition to feminism.

I am not sure if the men were genuinely more feminist oriented or if they were more wary of what they said to a woman interviewer on tape. In either case, most of the men gave answers similar to those of David. When I asked him if the empowerment of women was just as important as the uplifting of men to the cause of black liberation, he responded "Sure. We need everybody." When I asked if there was sexism in the black community, David said that there most definitely was. Finally, when I asked if black women should be feminists, he replied, "Feminism is for all women, and I think black women have suffered a lot of sexism." Although the men rather consistently espoused feminist ideas, none of them were willing to label themselves as feminists.

In sum, most members did not consider black men more oppressed than black women, and they believed that black men visited sexist oppression upon black women. Nevertheless, several agreed that feminism placed an undue double burden upon African American men who were fighting racism. In addition, most of the women rejected feminism for not speaking to their particular needs as black and religious women, as they were unfamiliar with the ways in which black feminism and womanism did speak in those ways.

Consequently, I suggest that within First Afrikan, the identification with womanism is not hindered by the androcentric and antifeminist rhetoric associated with black empowerment movements, as I found little evidence of such among this congregation. Rather, the main culprit appears to be the lack of education on black feminism and womanism offered to the members, who indicate an openness to a feminist critique that privileges their racial and Christian experiences. Evidence for this is provided by an encounter shortly after Elder Toure led a seminar on womanist theology. Carmen, who had previously stated that

she was unfamiliar with womanism and did not consider herself feminist, made a point to seek me out. Laughing, she said that she realized
why I had looked somewhat confused during our interview, as she was
plainly articulating feminist and womanist perspectives but denying
that she was either one. Because of the class with Elder Toure, Carmen
explained that she now realized that she had been a womanist all along
but did not know it.

Gendered Beliefs

Another impediment to the development of womanism identified by
Elder Toure was the proclivity for Afrocentric communities to ideal-
ize patriarchal African gender dynamics. She points out that there is
no one African culture but numerous African cultures, and, frequently,
women held and hold prominent roles of power within both the family and the public spheres. Other black feminists have critiqued Afrocentric ideology for focusing on those African cultural traditions that
privilege male dominance and for ignoring the influence of European
models of patriarchy on contemporary African cultural groups (Collins
1998; White 2001).

Many Afrocentric communities advocate gender complementarity or the concept that men and woman have different yet interdepen-
dent responsibilities within marriage and family life. Complementarity
reflects a patriarchal perspective in that men, as husbands and fathers,
are the leaders while women, as wives and mothers, support the men's
decisions. The argument is that the husband and wife roles enhance
and balance one another. Consequently, if women were to assume male
roles and responsibilities, this would result in confusion and imbalance
within the family. From this perspective, family stability and, by extension, the overall well-being of the black community is dependent upon
each member of the family attending to his or her specific gendered
roles and duties.

It is important to note that gender complementarity not only has its
basis within certain interpretations of African gender dynamics but also
within some interpretations of biblical gender dynamics. For instance, in 1
Cor. 11:3, it reads, "But I want you to understand that the head of every man
is Christ, the head of a wife is her husband, and the head of Christ is God."

Biblical passages such as this are employed to argue that God ordains the man to lead the family and commands the woman to be subservient to her husband. The husband's decisions for his family are to favor biblical ethics, and he is expected to protect and love his wife and children. By cooperating with, respecting, and supporting her husband, the woman assures that the family unit is balanced and in accordance with the will of God.

Those who espouse this view assert that complementarity does not advocate inequality between the genders, as the woman's role is considered just as valuable as the man's. The Afrocentric perspective is that African culture values motherhood and that it is only through a Eurocentric and feminist reading of motherhood that it is considered a lesser status than that of fatherhood (Bell 1990). Through complementarity, "the woman is revered in her role as the mother who is the bringer of life, the conduit for spiritual regeneration of the ancestors, the bearer of culture and the center of social organization" (Dove 1998: 520).

Gender complementarity meshes quite nicely with patriarchal black empowerment perspectives. Patricia Hill Collins points out that "gender complementarity dovetails with an ethic of service in which Black women and men exhibit racial solidarity by submerging their individual needs, goals and concerns to those of the Black community as a collectivity" (1998: 173). In addition, men are positioned as the moral leaders and thus able to reverse the ways in which the larger racist society has robbed them of their status and power. Also, gender complementarity resolves the problems associated with a black matriarchy as women are returned to their rightful status. Black women who put aside feminist notions of equality and embrace gender complementarity do not emasculate black men with matriarchal behaviors and thus nurture the larger community.

Those who critique gender complementarity note that it limits women's choices with rigid gender norms and that it awards men most of the social, political, and economic power as the decision makers. Another criticism is that by idealizing the imagined African past, gender complementarity does not attend to the contemporary needs and gender dynamics of families in either Africa or in African America. In addition, within both African-centered and religious defenses of complementarity there is evidence of cherry-picking or the practice of emphasizing some data while ignoring information that contradicts the stated position. For instance, in Ephesians, the Bible tells enslaved persons to obey their masters; few would advocate such a position today. Within some ancient and contemporary African cultures, husbands are allowed to beat their wives. Is this patriarchal practice to be adopted as well?

Barbara Ransby and Tracye Matthews posit that gender complementarity is not the separate but equal stance it claims to be. Rather, "unequal gender roles are redefined euphemistically as complementary rather than as the relationships of subordination and domination" they truly are (1995: 59). Furthermore, she argues that, if African America is "to ever realize a society where men and women are equally respected, valued and empowered, we have to step outside of traditional roles. We have to move beyond imposed, and often artificial, notions of family, parenting and sexuality and find the courage to create new definitions of both manhood and womanhood and how the two relate to one another (Ransby 2000: 220).

Head of Household

As First Afrikan is an Afrocentric and Christian community, I inquired into the member's attitudes concerning gender complementarity. One of the interviews was with Nina and Jerome, a young couple married for three years. I asked them to agree or disagree with the following statement: Women should not do the same things as men as they are made by nature to function differently.

> JEROME: I agree only because I don't believe that either role is better or worse. I feel like one cannot exist without the other. Remember, we were just saying this yesterday. We were watching "So You Can Dance," and she was like, "Does the man always have to lead the dance," and I was like, "Yeah, that's the way it is but because the women is in charge of all the flash and the grandeur of it all and without the two, it doesn't look right and it doesn't flow right, you know. The man is boring, the women make it look good."
>
> NINA: Yeah, I said, I can deal with that.
>
> JEROME: Yeah, but the man is the stiff one, is the one that controls—you know, not controls, but just guides it, you know what I'm saying. So

I feel like it's ying and yang. One cannot really be complete or whole without the other.

I asked Nina if she agreed with everything Jerome said. In part, I wanted to make sure I heard her opinion, and, in addition, I was curious about her response to his model of woman as style and man as control. Nina agreed with Jerome that gender relationships should have complementarity as men and women have different attributes. I pushed a bit further and asked both if they agreed that the man was the head of the household.

NINA: We talked about that, didn't we?

JEROME: Let's see here, do I want to answer this first? You go first.

NINA: I'm . . . he is. Well, the man represents the family. He does, and the woman—she represents the family, too. But the woman is also there to be his strength, you know. He has a lot of strength, you know, without the woman, but she's the driving force out there.

JEROME: Yes, a man may be the figurehead, but he ain't nothing, he's nothing without that woman at home.

NINA: He said it, not me.

JEROME: Nothing, he's nothing without the woman at home, you know, that's it.

NINA: He needs support and he needs reassurance when he comes home [from] the world.

JEROME: And you know, now that women are not homebodies, you know, they're out in the world, too. So they need just as much support as a man does, so it's really neck and neck.

Interestingly, while Nina said that a man was the head of the household, Jerome minimized the status by referring to it as a figurehead. And when Nina spoke of having to support the man after a long day in the world, it was Jerome who pointed out that women worked as well and also needed such support. His responses reminded me of a conversation with Reverend Lomax, who insisted to me that the men of the church were actually more feminist than the women and that he received the most resistance from his progressive ideologies from women. I had dismissed his claim until reviewing my field notes, and now I wish that I had paid more attention to that dynamic. Indeed, it was the women moreso than the men who agreed that the man should be the head of the household.

Hadiya, an unmarried woman in her thirties, agreed that the man should be the head of the household. "Yes, I think that. I agree, but he has to be God centered. I mean you just can't follow any man just because he's male. If he's God centered and has God at the forefront, then I think you can trust his decision to be—to make decisions as the head of the household because he's accountable. But you can't just follow a fool." Denise, in her late forties and married for fifteen years, concurred. However, she allowed for the fact that single mothers are often the de facto heads of household, and that because of changing social mores, women are more likely to be the final decision makers:

> In a family unit where there is a mother and a father present, I do believe that the male is head of the household. But in a household where the two are not married, if it's the female's home, then of course, the female is the head of the household there. That's hard. That's a very difficult one for me, but I certainly believe that men are the head of the family—somebody has to be the head of the household. Now, in some cases, I know the roles change, and the roles differ. And if there is agreement between the female and the male that the female be the head of the household, then I don't see a problem with that. But I do see, I do feel, that somebody needs to be head.

Although Denise considered it the ideal for the husband to be the head of household, in the end, she did express comfort with the wife being the head if both parties were amenable. Like Denise, most of my respondents, male and female, seemed to think that someone had to act as the head of the family. This is interesting, as much of the rhetoric by the members concerning the Afrocentric approach to decision making is that things should not be hierarchical but egalitarian. It was only in reference to male-female dynamics that respondents were to prefer hierarchy over corporate decision making. Also of note, although nearly half of the women to whom I posed the question agreed that the man should be the head of the household, only one of the women had an issue with the husband taking care of the children while the woman was the primary breadwinner. None of the men had a problem with this reversal of traditional roles. In fact, most did not believe the man must be the head of household, although they agreed that someone must take the leadership role.

Inherently Different

A corollary of gender complementarity is that women and men are made by nature to function differently. David, a single man in his forties, responded:

> I disagree with that. Yes, they are made differently biologically, but I think a woman should be able to do whatever a woman wants to do, just like I think men should do what men want to do. Because when I talk to young people, you tell them be your best and go out there and do your thing. And if your thing is to drive a race car for NASCAR, as a black female, great, I'll buy a ticket and come see you.

Asmina agreed with David, taking the argument further with the contention that patriarchy had warped social expectations of men and women:

> I think that men and women should do whatever their destinies demand they do. I think the Creator gives us each a destiny, a purpose, and it depends on your purpose. I think that rigid gender roles are born out of patriarchy, and it's another form of oppression. Certainly I think that women are biologically made to have babies and to nurse babies, but I also think fathers are biologically made to comfort babies. Have you ever noticed how little children—and this is true of me, I'm a forty-eight-year-old woman, but I love to put my head on my husband's chest when he's talking because the sound of his voice, that deep sound resonates with me. And that's true of little children, too.

Only four people, all women, agreed that nature intended for men and women to do different tasks. Felicia felt that women and men were made by nature to function differently, and what made them different was "just instinct, just knowing, women have that sense of knowing.

Also, we can, we have a sense of tasks. We can do three or four things where males can only focus on one." Denise also agreed, stating, "Certainly because we weren't made to do the same things is because the way our bodies [are made]. But they do not necessarily have to do with differences in our minds and the way we think." Hadiya thought that the only real difference was that men were physically stronger. These responses suggested that the only differences that made a difference were physical ones and those concerning temperament. No one cited a difference in intelligence.

In sum, while a significant number of participants advocated gender complementarity, only four believed that nature intended for women and men to perform different tasks. When defending complementarity, most explanations privileged biblical interpretations, none suggested it as a remedy to the racial oppression endured by black men, and only one person cited the traditional African family structure. This young woman, Subira, approached me on several occasions to use my anthropological expertise to educate the congregation about polygamy. When I asked her why, she explained that there were not enough good black men for the black women who needed husbands and that this traditional African practice could resolve the problem. Personally uncomfortable with any woman embracing polygamy in which a man has several wives, I asked Subira if she was not concerned about women sharing a husband and if she saw no problem in several women catering to one man. She responded that the African family structure required the man to take care of all of the wives equally and that women were naturally suited to taking care of men and children. As I did not want to critique Subira's beliefs any further, I did my best to avoid her and demurred whenever she caught up with me.

Conclusion

The attitudes toward womanist thought at First Afrikan reflect the employment of the theology as counterdiscourse and highlight the barriers of moving from feminist theory to practice. Just as the church used Afrocentric and black liberation theologies to oppose and invalidate Eurocentric theological discourse, womanist theological perspectives were adopted to challenge the legitimacy of patriarchal readings of the

Bible. Both men and women were open to biblical interpretations and liturgical dynamics that privileged the perspectives of women. Moreover, women members, in particular, spoke of feeling affirmed and validated by the feminist language and womanist theology espoused by the church leadership. In fact, for many women, the church was one of the first and few spaces in which these perspectives were encouraged and sanctioned.

However, although both women and men employed womanist language and claimed antipatriarchal, antiandrocentric, and antisexist viewpoints, few of them identified as "feminist," "black feminist," or "womanist." Those members who were comfortable referring to themselves as either "feminist" or "womanist" did so before joining the church. Those disinclined to use the labels received little to no pressure to do otherwise. Although the leadership of the church deliberately incorporated womanist theology and language into their sermons and teachings, they did not as zealously encourage members to identify as womanist, as they did for them to identify as Afrocentric.

According to Elder Toure, the leadership worried that members would be unable or reluctant to develop their womanist consciousness in tandem with their African-centered consciousness. In addition, she was also concerned with the sustainability of meaningful changes in gendered behavior. Elder Toure doubted that there were sufficiently safe spaces within the church and congregants' lives to experiment with womanist-inspired interactions between women and men. Specifically, she cited the androcentric tenor of black empowerment movements and the patriarchal leanings of Afrocentric ideologies as a hindrance to such behavioral changes.

Congregants' attitudes suggest that this particular Black Nationalist community did not privilege the perspectives of men and thus eschewed androcentrism moreso than did their historical counterparts. In contrast, a significant number did endorse a patriarchal gender complementarity. Interestingly though, they cited their Christian, not Afrocentric, beliefs for these opinions. However, one cannot ignore Subira's embrace of polygamy as an African-centered and positive practice.

Overall, the members' critiques of black liberation discourses that marginalized women and of feminist ideologies that did not attend to the black experience suggest that they would be open to more overtly identifying with a womanist theology that spoke to the intersectionality of racism and sexism and advocated the eradication of both. Furthermore, it is only with a deeper understanding of womanist ideology and practice that members will be able to begin negotiation for safe spaces in which to experiment with how these tenets might manifest in their relationships.

In *Gender Talk*, Cole and Guy-Sheftall raise two important questions in their consideration of the relationship between black empowerment and black feminism: "What would a vision of Black community transformation look life if gender were more central to our analytic frameworks? What might we learn from engaging in more systematic analyses of the struggles between race and gender within African American communities?" (2003: 73). I wonder what the answers to these questions might be if the leadership of First Afrikan were to advocate womanist theology and practice as rigorously and consistently as they do Afrocentric theology and practice. Furthermore, if taught in tandem, how might these two counterdiscourses inform one another and influence member identity, consciousness, and behavior?

Conclusion

The Benediction

Ashe Ashe Ashe O

A community is a group of people with common values who perceive themselves in some respect as distinct and who have a sense of social cohesion. At First Afrikan Presbyterian Church, community is based on the congregation's shared Christianity, Afrocentrism, middle class status, and blackness. The ideological tenets of their Afrocentric Christianity provide answers to the ontological questions, What are my origins? Who are my people? and What should be the values and practices that shape my life? Significantly, the intersection of race with class as well as varied interpretations of Afrocentrism provides multiple answers to each of these questions. At the same time, the church is able to sustain communitas, or its profound sensibility of solidarity, because of the belief that, despite the diversity among them, they are fundamentally and essentially unified through their common blackness and Africanness. In order to best understand this black, middle class, and Afrocentric church community, one must consider how they negotiate the tensions between heterogeneous and essentialist constructions of identity.

First Afrikan is a community in the process of creating an identity and nurturing a culture that privileges African ways of knowing and

being. In general, Afrocentrism purports to provide direction for identifying authentic African values and practicing authentic blackness. In
the specific case of First Afrikan, authentic Africanness and blackness
are each understood to be both immutable and in flux.

The church has established resolute tenets for how an African-centered person should think and act within the social contexts in which
she finds herself. At the same time, the church is a space that tolerates a
diversity of ideas and approaches to being an Afrocentric person. Consequently, this book has examined the interplay between the firmly held
convictions of the community and the continuum along which those
convictions are interpreted and enacted. By this, I mean that for any
one issue there is a range of varied perspectives and positionalities
within the congregation. At First Afrikan Presbyterian Church there are
multiple perspectives concerning what it means to be Afrocentric, middle class, gendered, and black. The commitment of the church members
to create and maintain community through a negotiation of these multiple ideas and positions is the crux of the book.

The leadership considers the church, among other things, a space
where one can learn about and celebrate African heritage and culture
as well as spiritually evolve with an appreciation of the connections
between Africanness and Christianity. However, members have joined
for reasons that do and do not speak to the hopes and desires of the
leadership. At one end of the continuum are those who visit First Afrikan because it is a predominantly black Presbyterian church close to
their homes; along the continuum are those who have no particular
interest in Afrocentrism but who enjoy the vitriolic political rhetoric
of Reverend Lomax; and at the other end are those who are invested in
living wholly Afrocentric lives. As a result, First Afrikan is an environment that harbors people of vastly different motivations, some of whom
are seeking to create a collective identity and others who are attending to their own personal needs. For those who are attempting to create a collective identity based on Afrocentrism, there is again unity and
difference.

Many scholars and pundits approach Afrocentrism as if it were a
singular phenomenon with a universal interpretation. First Afrikan
provides a clear refutation of this assumption in that within this one
Afrocentric environment there is no uniform consensus about what

Afrocentrism should look like, and the majority of the community is apparently of the opinion that how one constructs an Afrocentric identity is a matter of personal choice. For some members of the community, Afrocentrism is a consciousness, an awareness of the self as an African person, while for others, consciousness is only one facet of Afrocentric identity in that individuals are expected to behave in particularly African ways. A fully realized African consciousness is one that knows African history and culture and has internalized an African worldview, whereas Afrocentric behavior includes, but is not limited to, wearing African or African-inspired hairstyles and clothing, adopting African names, and speaking an African language. For some, Africa is a metaphysical space that serves as the seat of culture and history binding together those of African descent dispersed throughout the Diaspora, while for others, reference to Africa means the actual continent, the geographical space where one should be physically located in order to truly realize the self.

Critics have argued that Africa is appropriated by Afrocentric people without sufficient attention to the continent's social and cultural diversity both historically and contemporarily, and critics have taken issue with how Afrocentric communities arbitrarily decide what are and are not considered relevant African cultural mores, social customs, or even history. At First Afrikan Church, the crux of members' Afrocentrism is the creative remembering and rearranging of history and culture in order to create a coherent identity in which as many members as possible can share. This does not mean that the congregation fabricates history or does not make reasonable effort to appreciate the cultural complexity of the continent. Rather, as the task of incorporating all that is African is a monumental, if not impossible, task and as members are coming from widely varied backgrounds with just as varied motivations, the church has been deliberate in choosing those aspects of African culture and history that best speak to their current circumstances and that are flexible enough to be interpreted by a diverse group of individuals.

While the church is upfront about certain aspects of African history and culture being privileged over others for particular ends, nevertheless, some would be troubled by key moments when cultural complexity and diversity are erased within a discourse of universality. In ways that certainly vex detractors of Afrocentricity, the church promotes the notion that there are essential aspects of Africanness that transcend time and place and inhere in all persons or communities of African descent. This essentialized Africa meets several needs of the diverse community. For example, as most African Americans do not know the specific ethnic group or even country from which their ancestors hail, a construction of Africa that transcends these political boundaries provides a place with which to connect. Also, a universalized Africanness shared by biblical actors, ancient Egyptians, and contemporary peoples fosters a sense of historical greatness and glorious destiny as a people.

In addition to imagining Africanness in ways that foster a shared sense of identity, the church also recreates Africa in ways that deliberately speak to and against Eurocentric constructions. First Afrikan's construction of Africanness is an exercise in claiming autonomy for rendering members' history, culture, and identity within the public imagination as well as within their own. This can be seen most clearly in how the church reinterprets the Bible and the roles of Africanness and blackness within it. The reading of the Bible as an African text and the construction of biblical actors as black are critical aspects of identity construction for many church members. One may understand himself as a person of African descent with an especial responsibility to honor his relationship to a God sympathetic to blackness and a Jesus who is in fact black. Through this biblical interpretation, congregants shape an understanding of "who I am and whose I am."

The shared sense of identity based on an essentialized blackness juxtaposed to a hegemonic whiteness has resonance with this particular community as it provides a sense of communitas that is especially valuable to a group that may feel alienated. As well-educated and affluent members of the larger cultural and sociopolitical community of the United States, middle class African Americans have assimilated and performed those values and behaviors expected of socially mobile Americans. Yet, as black people, they see neither their phenotype nor ethnicity recognized or celebrated to the same degree as whiteness within either biblical or national discourses. Marginalized within the larger community, the Afrocentric community provides a space in which there are shared notions of what it means to be a good Christian, a loyal member of the nation, and a spouse with appropriate family values based on shared notions of blackness and Africanness rather than whiteness and Europeanness. To some extent, the Afrocentrism of middle class peoples is not a rejection of Eurocentrism but rather a reaction to Eurocentrism's rejection or, more accurately, marginalization of them. The intense feeling of social equality and solidarity flourishes within First Afrikan because it provides a space in which their particularly classed, gendered, and raced ways of being are privileged and celebrated.

The Afrocentrism practiced at First Afrikan employs essentialist constructions of blackness and Africanness in order to meet the needs of a community whose knowledge of its African origins has been fractured, whose sense of connection to Christianity has been undermined by Eurocentric biblical interpretations, and whose feelings of assimilation into the larger American culture are not fully realized despite their middle class status. This is a community struggling with feelings of disconnection from their ancestral, spiritual, and national moorings. Afrocentrism supplies not only explanations for this disconnect with arguments of deliberate marginalization of blackness and privileging of whiteness but also supplies the remedy with arguments of a transcendent and timeless blackness that naturally inheres in all people of African descent. Despite attempts of erasure and acts toward marginalization, Africanness and blackness will persist because, by their very nature, neither can be fundamentally altered. Within this Afrocentric discourse of essentialized identity is the powerful belief that, by connecting with such constructions, an individual will be able to realize his authentic self and a community will be able to employ this collective authenticity to empower itself. Essentialist constructions of an identity can be quite effective in fostering communitas based on shared narratives of struggle and strategies of relief. However, no person has a single axis of identity; rather, she understands herself and is understood by others to be positioned at the various intersections of multiple axes of identity.

Blackness, for example, intersects with middle class status. Feelings of communitas can be undermined as an individual struggles to decide who his community is or to manage his allegiance to multiple communities. Even if a person employed essentialist notions of blackness, Afrocentrism, and even middle classness, there is still the quandary of how to navigate all three positionalities simultaneously.

Middle class status at times conflicts with blackness as individuals worry that assimilation into middle class culture equates to assimilation into white culture and alienation from the larger black culture. In addition, for some, the status conflicts with Afrocentric thought as the materialism and conspicuous consumption associated with the bourgeoisie is perceived as antithetical to the communal and egalitarian ethos of Afrocentrism. These experiences of conflict mesh with DuBois's description of double consciousness as "two thoughts, two unreconciled strivings; two warring ideals in one dark body" (1903: 3). Afrocentrism offers a possible remedy to the two unreconciled strivings as constructions of blackness emphasize culture, in terms of Africanness, rather than class, associated with the poor. Furthermore, it is predicated on acts of conspicuous consumption, such as authentic African clothing and trips to African countries. This middle class Afrocentric reimagining of blackness attends to concerns of overidentification with whiteness and makes a place for affluence within the performance of identity.

Blackness can also conflict with constructions of Americanness. Reverend Lomax's sermons concerning Melchizedek put forth an understanding of African Americans as having an integrationist role in the American polity, while his critiques of President Bush advocated a separatist stance. As evidenced by the interviews with members of the congregation, black Americans are able to simultaneously feel a part of and apart from the American community. Middle class African Americans, in particular, are able to perform quintessential Americanness, such as appropriate choices in which schools to attend and careers to attain; speaking in the appropriate dialect; privileging the appropriate social values and mores; and appreciating the appropriate music, food, and clothing. The appropriate values and practices of Americanness are deeply associated with middle class whiteness. Simultaneously, middle class Black Americans are marginalized by acts of racism as well as the cultural pressure to distance themselves from cultural practices associated with poorer African Americans. Black Nationalism and Afrocentrism validate these feelings of cultural marginalization and suggest that the remedy is a cultural perspective that rejects whiteness and embraces blackness.

DuBois (1903) wrote that the remedy for double consciousness among African Americans required neither the Africanization of

America nor the whitening of the souls of black folk but rather the attainment of true African Americanness—or, in other words, the forging of a place of cultural belonging and sociopolitical integration for black people in the United States. The election of Barack Obama would seem to be the fulfillment of that prescription. However, a controversy during Obama's first campaign was his membership in Trinity United Church of Christ, a Black Nationalist and Afrocentric community. I do not presume to know his heart and mind, but his membership suggests that, despite his middle class status and degree of assimilation into the larger community, Obama nevertheless struggled with feelings of marginalization. The post-election contention among some European American citizens that they "need to take their America back from Obama" may certainly be evidence of the continued African American racialized exclusion from the larger American family.

Double consciousness depends, in part, on essentialist notions of Americanness, middle classness, and blackness. An essentialized Americanness requires whiteness, and an essentialized middle class identity is necessarily juxtaposed to less-affluent values and practices, whereas an essentialized blackness depends upon the presumed cultural authenticity of poorer African Americans. These dynamics reveal the power of essentialist constructions of identity. The positionality and resultant experiences and perspectives of First Afrikan's members demonstrate the power of heterogeneous constructions of identity to destabilize essentialized ones.

These middle class black Americans cannot fit comfortably into any of the above essentialized constructions, hence their experiences of double consciousness and membership in an Afrocentric church. Discourses concerning Afrocentric biblical interpretations, middle class angst, the inclusion of womanist theology, and ambivalence concerning Americanness are evidence of efforts to manage allegiances to competing groups because of the varied intersections of their axes of identity. Importantly, however, the members of First Afrikan are not mired betwixt and between these essentialist constructions. Rather, they are actively privileging and negotiating the intersections of blackness with middle class status, gender identity, and Americanness.

The communitas fostered at First Afrikan Presbyterian Church is based just as much on the privileging of heterogeneity among its members as it is upon the essentialist constructions of blackness. The discourses that contend that both middle class and less-affluent constructions of blackness are equally valid, that advocate the especial responsibility of Afrocentric Christians to the larger American community, and that seek to reconcile Black Nationalist and black feminist ideologies speak to the shared investment in a community that is simultaneously and successfully middle class and black and American. Furthermore, the collective sensibility that they are distinct from others and share common values and allegiances is primarily founded on their belief in a shared blackness, a blackness that is essentially the same and simultaneously diverse in how it is experienced. If community is a key site in which an individual comes to know who he is by identifying who his people are, I contend that the members believe that they belong at First Afrikan because it is a gathering of individuals who foster solidarity by privileging difference.

The members of First Afrikan Presbyterian Church experience blackness in multiple ways. There is a blackness interconnected with an African-centered consciousness, a blackness associated with poorer African Americans and another with middle class African Americans, a blackness tainted by too close an association to whiteness as well as one aspiring parity with whiteness, a blackness that embraces Americanness and a blackness that emphasizes alienation from Americanness, and a blackness that imagines itself as an oppressed status and a blackness that imagines itself as a chosen people of God. The congregants are at times comfortable with the heterogeneous nature of their black identity and at other times experience consternation and confusion with its multiplicity.

The multiplicity and seeming contradiction do not reflect confusion about what blackness is but rather speak to the fluid and adaptable ways in which the identity is employed.

Within this community, the members are struggling to understand and negotiate, as individuals and a collective, their current situation and destiny as religious, cultural, and racial actors. Blackness is used to construct what it means to be a Christian, what it means to be person of African descent, what it means to be a citizen of the United States, what it means to be middle class, and what it means to be an Afrocentric man or woman. Stretched in so many directions, it is inevitable that there would be such a proliferation of constructions of blackness. In addition, as other positionalities such as religion, gender, and class are filtered through blackness in the service of individual and collective identity construction, it is also inevitable that blackness would contain the dynamics of both essentialism and heterogeneity. In fact, the discourses and practices within First Afrikan Presbyterian Church demonstrate that much of the power of blackness comes from the interplay between these two dynamics. Through a description and analysis of the ways in which this community defines, performs, and lives black identity, we glean a deeper understanding and richer appreciation of the multihued and dynamic phenomenon that is blackness.

REFERENCES

Adeleke, Tunde. 1998. "Black Americans and Africa: A Critique of the Pan-African and Identity Paradigms." *International Journal of African Historical Studies* 31(3):505–536.

———. 2001. "Will the Real Father of Afrocentricity Please Stand." *Western Journal of Black Studies* 25(1):21–29.

Ani, Marimba. 1994. *Yurugu: An African-Centered Critique of European Cultural Thought and Behavior.* Trenton, NJ: Africa World Press.

Asante, Molefi Kete. 1991. "The Afrocentric Idea in Education." *Journal of Negro Education* 60(2):170–180.

———. 1998. *The Afrocentric Idea.* Philadelphia: Temple University Press.

Austin, Algernon. 2006. *Achieving Blackness: Race, Black Nationalism and Afrocentrism in the Twentieth Century.* New York: New York University Press.

Baer, Hans A., and Merrill Singer. 2002. *African American Religion: Varieties of Protest and Accommodation.* Knoxville: University of Tennessee Press.

Barth, Fredrik. 1969. *Ethnic Groups and Boundaries: The Social Organization of Culture Difference.* Oslo: Universitetsforlaget.

Bell, Yvonne R. 1990. "Afrocentric Cultural Consciousness and African-American Male-Female Relationships." *Journal of Black Studies* 2(2):162–189.

Brown, Kelly Delaine Douglas. 2003. "Womanist Theology: What Is Its Relationship to Black Theology?" In *Black Theology: A Documentary History.* Ed. James H. Cone and Gayraud S. Wilmore, 290–299. Maryknoll, NY: Orbis Books.

Brown, Michael Joseph. 2004. *Blackening the Bible: The Aims of African American Biblical Scholarship.* New York: Trinity Press International.

Bruner, Edward M. 1996. "Tourism in Ghana: The Representation of Slavery and the Return of the Black Diaspora." *American Anthropologist* 98(2):290–304.

Clifford, James. 1994. "Diasporas." *Cultural Anthropology* 9(3):302–338.

Cobb, Jr., William. 1997. "Out of Africa: The Dilemmas of Afrocentricity." *Journal of Negro History* 82(1):122–132.

Cole, Johnnetta, and Beverly Guy-Sheftall. 2003. *Gender Talk: The Struggle for Women's Equality in African American Communities.* New York: Ballantine Books.

Coleman, Will. 1994. *Tribal Talk: Black Theology, Hermeneutics and African/American Ways of Telling the Story*. University Park: Pennsylvania State University Press.

Collins, Patricia Hill. 1998. *Fighting Words: Black Women and the Search for Justice*. Minnesota: University of Minnesota Press.

———. 2006. *From Black Power to Hip Hop: Racism, Nationalism and Feminism*. Philadelphia: Temple University Press.

Combahee River Collective. 1995. "A Black Feminist Statement." In *Words of Fire: An Anthology of African American Feminist Thought*. Ed. Beverly Guy-Sheftall. New York: New Press.

Cone, James H. 1992. *Martin and Malcolm and America: A Dream or a Nightmare*. Maryknoll, NY: Orbis Books.

Dawson, Michael C. 2003. *Black Visions: The Roots of Contemporary African-American Political Ideologies*. Chicago: University of Chicago Press.

Delany, Martin. 1880. *Principia of Ethnology: The Origin of Races and Color, with an Archeological Compendium of Ethiopian and Egyptian Civilization*. Montana: Keesinger Publishing.

Dove, Nah. 1998. "African Womanism: An Afrocentric Theory." *Journal of Black Studies* 28(5):515–539.

Drake, St. Clair. 1990. *Black Folk Here and There: An Essay in History and Anthropology*. Los Angeles: University of California Press.

DuBois, W. E. B. 1897. "The Conservation of the Races." *American Negro Academy Occasional Papers*, no. 2. Washington, DC: American Negro Academy.

———. 1903. *The Souls of Black Folk: Essays and Sketches*. Chicago: McClurg & Co.

Durant, Thomas, and Kathleen Sparrow. 1997. "Race and Class Consciousness among Lower- and Middle-Class Blacks." *Journal of Black Studies* 27(3):334–351.

Early, Gerald. 1999. "Adventures in the Colored Museum: Afrocentrism, Memory, and the Construction of Race." *American Anthropologist* 100(3):703–711.

Frazier, E. Franklin. 1957. *Black Bourgeoise: The Rise of a New Middle Class*. New York: Free Press.

Greenlee, Sam. 1969. *The Spook Who Sat by the Door*. Detroit, MI: Wayne State University Press.

Gudmundson, Lowell, and Justin Wolfe, eds. 2010. *Blacks and Blackness in Central America: Between Race and Place*. Durham, NC: Duke University Press.

Hall, Carol Lynnette. 1994. "The Middle Class African American Home: Its Objects and Their Meanings." Ph.D. dissertation, Sociology Department, Iowa State University.

Hansen, Karen Tranberg. 2004. "The World in Dress: Anthropological Perspectives on Clothing, Fashion and Culture." *Annual Review of Anthropology* 33:369–392.

Harris-Lacewell, Melissa. 2004. *Barbershops, Bibles and BET: Everyday Talk and Black Political Thought*. Princeton, NJ: Princeton University Press.

Harrison, Faye. 1995. *The Persistent Power of Race in the Cultural and Political Economy of Racism. Annual Review of Anthropology* 33:369–392.

Hartigan, John. 2010. *Race in the Twenty-First Century: Ethnographic Approaches.* Oxford: Oxford University Press.

Hernandez-Reguant, Ariana. 1999. "Kwanzaa and the US Ethnic Mosaic." In *Representations of Blackness and the Performance of Identities.* Ed. Jean Muteba Rahier, 120–132. Westport, CT: Bergin & Garvey.

Hobsbawm, Eric, and Terrence Ranger. 1983. *The Invention of Tradition.* Cambridge: Cambridge University Press.

Hope Felder, Cain. 2003. "Cultural Ideology, Afrocentrism and Biblical Interpretation." In *Black Theology: A Documentary History.* Ed. James H. Cone and Gayraud S. Wilmore, 184–195. Maryknoll, NY: Orbis Books.

Hopkins, Dwight, and Thomas, Linda E. 2001. "Black Theology USA Revisited." *Journal of Theology for Southern Africa* 100(1):61–85.

Hudson-Weems, Clenora. 2006. *Africana Womanism: Reclaiming Ourselves.* Troy, MI: Bedford Publishing.

Jackson, John L., Jr. 2005. *Real Black: Adventures in Racial Sincerity.* Chicago: University of Chicago Press.

Johnson, Sylvester A. 2010. "The Rise of Black Ethnics: The Ethnic Turn in African American Religions, 1916–1945." *Religion and American Culture: A Journal of Interpretation* 20(2):125–163.

Lacy, Karyn. 2007. *Blue Chip Black: Race, Class and Status in the New Black Middle Class.* Los Angeles: University of California Press.

Lomax, Mark A. 1995. "The Effects of an Afrocentric Hermeneutic in a Developing Congregation." Ph.D. dissertation, United Theological Seminary.

———. 2002. "First Afrikan Presbyterian Church New Members' Class Study Book." Atlanta: First Afrikan Presbyterian Church.

Markey, Eileen. 2008. "Liberation Theology Frames Wright's View." *National Catholic Reporter,* April 4.

Martin, Ben L. 1991. "From Negro to Black to African American: The Power of Names and Naming." *Political Science Quarterly* 106(1):83–107.

May, Reuben A. Buford. 2001. *Talking at Trena's: Everyday Conversations at an African American Tavern.* New York: New York University Press.

Moses, Wilson J. 1998. *Afrotopia: The Roots of African American Popular History.* Cambridge: Cambridge University Press.

Moynihan, Patrick. 1965. "The Negro Family: The Case for National Action." Washington, DC: U.S. Department of Labor, Office of Policy Planning and Research.

Phillips, Layli. 2006. *The Womanist Reader.* New York: Routledge.

Price, Melanye. 2009. *Dreaming Blackness: Black Nationalism and African American Public Opinion.* New York: New York University Press.

Raboteau, Albert J. 2001. *Canaan Land: A Religious History of African Americans.* New York: Oxford University Press.

Ransby, Barbara. 2000. "Afrocentrism, Cultural Nationalism, and the Problem with Essentialist Definitions of Race, Gender, and Sexuality." In *Dispatches from the*

Ebony Tower: Intellectuals Confront the African American Experience. Ed. Manning Marable. New York: Columbia University Press.

Ransby, Barbara, and Tracye Matthews. 1995. "Black Popular Culture and the Transcendence of Patriarchal Illusions." In *Words of Fire: An Anthology of African American Feminist Thought.* Ed. Beverly Guy-Sheftall, 526–536. New York: New Press.

Rath, Richard Cullen. 1997. "Echo and Narcissus: The Afrocentric Pragmatism of W. E. B. DuBois." *Journal of American History* 84(2):461–495.

Robinson, Dean E. 2001. *Black Nationalism in American Politics and Thought.* Cambridge: Cambridge University Press.

Ross, Doran H. 1998. *Wrapped in Pride: Ghanaian Kente and African American Identity.* Los Angeles: Fowler Museum of Cultural History, University of California, Los Angeles.

Russell, Paitra D. 2002. "Styling Blackness: African American Hair Styling Practices in Late Twentieth Century America and the Phenomenology of Race." Ph.D. dissertation, Department of Anthropology, University of Chicago.

Sansone, Livio. 2003. *Blackness without Ethnicity: Constructing Race in Brazil.* New York: Palgrave MacMillan.

Smedley, Audrey. 2011. *Race in North America: Origin and Evolution of a Worldview.* Boulder, CO: Westview Press.

Smith, Tom W. 1992. "Changing Racial Labels: From Colored to Negro to Black to African American." *Public Opinion Quarterly* 56(4):496–514.

Speller, Julia. 2005. *Walkin' the Talk: Keepin' the Faith in Africentric Congregations.* Cleveland, OH: Pilgrim Press.

Springer, Kimberly. 2005. *Living for the Revolution: Black Feminist Organizations, 1968–1980.* Durham, NC: Duke University Press.

Stoller, Paul 2002. *Money Has No Smell: The Africanization of New York City.* Chicago: University of Chicago Press.

Sturm, Circe. 2011. *Becoming Indian: The Struggle over Cherokee Identity in the Twenty-First Century.* Santa Fe, NM: School for Advanced Research Press.

Telles, Edward. 2006. *Race in Another America: The Significance of Skin Color in Brazil.* Princeton, NJ: Princeton University Press.

Trevor-Roper, Hugh. 1983. "The Invention of Tradition: The Highland Tradition of Scotland." In *The Invention of Tradition.* Ed. Eric Hobsbawm and Terrence Ranger, 15–42. Cambridge: Cambridge University Press.

Turner, Victor W. 1969. *The Ritual Process: Structure and Anti-structure.* Chicago: Aldine Publishing Co.

Vanneman, Reeve. 1987. *The American Perception of Class.* Philadelphia: Temple University Press.

Walker, Alice. 1983. *In Search of Our Mothers' Gardens: Womanist Prose.* San Diego: Harcourt Brace Jovanovich.

Warms, Richard. 2009. *Sacred Realms: Readings in the Anthropology of Religion.* Oxford: Oxford University Press.

Waters, Mary C. 2001. *Black Identities: West Indian Immigrant Dreams and American Realities*. Cambridge, MA: Harvard University Press.

White, Frances. 2001. "Africa on My Mind: Gender, Counter Discourse and African American Nationalism." In *Is It Nation Time: Contemporary Essays on Black Power and Black Nationalism*. Ed. Eddie Glaude, 120–132. Chicago: University of Chicago Press.

Wilkins, Amy. 2008. *Wannabes, Goths and Christians: The Boundaries of Sex, Style and Status*. Chicago: University of Chicago Press.

Williams, Delores. 1993. *Sisters in the Wilderness: The Challenge of Womanist God-Talk*. New York: Orbis.

———. 1995. "Afrocentrism and Male-Female Relations in Church and Society." In *Living the Intersection: Womanism and Afrocentrism in Theology*. Ed. Cheryl Sanders. Minneapolis: Fortress Press.

Wilson, William Julius. 1978. *The Declining Significance of Race: Blacks and Changing American Institutions*. Chicago: University of Chicago Press.

Wolf, Eric. 1994. "Perilous Ideas: Race, Culture and People." *Current Anthropology* 35(1):1–12.

Wright, Jeremiah. 2003. "Doing Black Theology in the Black Church." In *Living Stones in the Household of God: The Legacy and Future of Black Theology*. Ed. Linda E. Thomas, 13–23. Minneapolis, MN: Fortress Press.

———. 2007. "Words from the Pulpit: Faith in a Foreign Land." *CrossCurrents* (Summer): 237–251.

INDEX

Africa, 62–64

African/Africanness: and the Bible, 76–77; and blackness, 79, 94–96; and God, 73; identity politics and, 60–62

African Diaspora, defined, 85

African Hebrew Israelites, 36

Afrocentric: consciousness, 45–46; dress, 50–53; hairstyles, 53–56; naming practices, 56–62, theology, 91

Afrocentrism, 10–13; defined, 25; and black middle class, 119–121, 123–124, 170–173; and Christianity, 74; history of, 25–27; and relationship to blackness, 8; tenets of, 27–29

Ancestral memory, 91–93, 141

Becoming Indian, 65–69

Biblical blackness, 89–91, 94

Black culture, 82–85

Black feminism, defined, 143–144

Black Liberation Theology, tenets of, 75–77, 89

Black Nationalism: defined, 126–127; First Afrikan Presbyterian attitudes toward, 131–135

Blackness: defined, 9; and Africanness, 79; of biblical characters, 89–91; characteristics and experiences of, 5–9; and collective identity, 85–87; cross-cultural constructions of, 77–87; degrees of, 101–107, 176–177; First Afrikan Presbyterian constructions of, 87; and First African Presbyterian, defined by, 96–100

Blue Chip Black, 118–119

Bush, George W., 129

Communitas: defined, 18; and blackness, 19–20; at First Afrikan Presbyterian, 172–173, 175

Double consciousness: defined, 7; and black theology, 75; defined in *Souls of Black Folk*, 125; 174–175; and middle class status, 21

Dreaming Blackness, 136

Essentialism: defined, 8, 19, 100; and blackness, 10, 172–173, 175–177; and heterogeneity, 9; and identity, 66, 97

Eurocentrism: defined, 10–11, 172–173

Feminism: defined, 143; perspectives of First Afrikan Presbyterian members, 157–160

First Afrikan Presbyterian Church: constructions of blackness, 87; definitions of blackness, 96–100; defining characteristics of, 7; history of, 29–31; middle class status of members, 112; perspectives on feminism, 157–160; perspectives on womanism, 158–160

Gender complementarity, 160–165

Gender Talk, 153; 168

Ideology, 16–17

Kiswahili, defined, 74

Maafa, defined, 74

McKinney, Cynthia, and Condoleeza Rice, 104–107

Middle class status: and Afrocentrism, 119–121; black, characteristics of, 112–113; black middle class, social science theories of, 117–119; black, relationship to Afrocentrism, 123–124, 174–175; and First Afrikan Presbyterian members, 112

ABOUT THE AUTHOR

Andrea C. Abrams is Assistant Professor of Anthropology, Gender Studies, and African American Studies at Centre College in Danville, Kentucky.